A Workbook For Leaders

AGILE BY
CHOICE

LUKAS MICHEL

ADVANCE PRAISE

"*Agile by Choice* is an eye opener for executives looking for a way to manage organizations in a very complex environment; it gives a fresh, new perspective on the mental shift required to be successful in managing work and people in turbulent times. This book will change the way you look at organizational agility."

Sergio Seanez, CEO, Foundamentality, Mexico Stadt, Mexico

"With Lukas Michel's books on the Performance Triangle, I was always able to help clients find successful solutions for their managerial and organizational challenges. His new book, *Agile by Choice*, offers the diagnostics and exercises that make my coaching a high return on investment engagement."

Richard Burgener, Managing Director, BURGENER & PARTNER Management Consulting, Bitch, Switzerland

"*Agile by Choice* offers a deep-dive into agile and beyond. The many exercises will help you on your individual path to get there fast. The book bridges individual and organizational agility in an unparalleled manner. Make it your book."

Dr Christoph Peter, Executive Director Digital Insurance, University of St Gall, Switzerland

"*Agile by Choice* provides a masterful roadmap, in the form of thought-provoking, practical, and insightful support and tools, allowing leaders to make significant changes in short timespans. A rare, different, and compelling book. Hugely recommendable."

Ana Maria Zumstein, Customer Experience Expert, Zurich Insurance Company, Zürich, Switzerland

Published by
LID Publishing Limited
The Record Hall, Studio 304,
16-16a Baldwins Gardens,
London EC1N 7RJ, UK

info@lidpublishing.com
www.lidpublishing.com

A member of:

businesspublishersroundtable.com

© Lukas Michel, 2021
© LID Publishing Limited, 2021

Printed by Severn, Gloucester

ISBN: 978-1-911671-06-0
ISBN: 978-1-911671-46-6 (ebook)

Cover and page design: Caroline Li

A Workbook For Leaders

AGILE BY
CHOICE

LUKAS MICHEL

MADRID | MEXICO CITY | LONDON
NEW YORK | BUENOS AIRES
BOGOTA | SHANGHAI | NEW DELHI

CONTENTS

Acknowledgments   1

Foreword   2

Preface   4

CHAPTER 1: BUSINESS CHALLENGES   10

     My Self

     Expectations

     Strategy

     Operating Modes

     Success

CHAPTER 2: FIVE LEADERSHIP DIMENSIONS   34

     #1   People

     #2   Organization

     #3   Management

     #4   Work

     #5   Operations

CHAPTER 3: THE INNER GAME   90

     Inner and Outer Interactions

     Playing the Inner Game

     Flow

     Awareness

     Choice

     Trust

CHAPTER 4: RESOURCES   132

     Energy

     Focus of Attention

     Time

     Space

CHAPTER 5: DECISIONS   168
    Productive Operating Environments
    Implementing Agile Decision-Making

CHAPTER 6: LEADERSHIP EVERYWHERE   184

CHAPTER 7: EXPERIENTIAL LEARNING   200

TOOLS   212
  #1   The Virus Check
  #2   My Challenge Map
  #3   Take a Break
  #4   Agile Diagnostic
  #5   Review Stakeholders
  #6   Document Agile
  #7   Get into the Flow
  #8   Create Awareness
  #9   It's Your Choice
 #10   Examine Trust
 #11   Review Commitment
 #12   Check Your Energy
 #13   Refuel Your Energy
 #14   Pay Attention
 #15   Time Accounts
 #16   101 on Executive Time
 #17   Pace Your Time
 #18   Executive Pace
 #19   Accountability Profile
 #20   Make Your Choice
 #21   Start with Your Team

Notes   258
Bibliography   259
List of Illustrations   261
About the Author   263
Book Summary   264

To the mentoring members of the
AGILITYINSIGHTS network.

ACKNOWLEDGMENTS

Agile by Choice goes back 20 years to the roots of my first inner game experiences, which were on skiing. Later, I practised the same with golf. More and more, the idea of the inner game influenced my work with the AGILITYINSIGHTS network and our diagnostic solutions. It was always about raising higher awareness, trust in capabilities, the choice to let things go and focus of attention.

In that sense, my deepest thanks go to my teacher and friend Dr Roberto Buner, owner of www.flowstate.ch and AGILITYINSIGHTS certified mentor. He introduced me to the inner game with his workshops on skiing. His exercises truly opened my eyes to an area that had been hidden to me before. Thank you. We will continue to practice our inner game on skiing, with golf and with our clients. It's so valuable for today's dynamic era.

My thanks also go to all 35 members of our AGILITYINSIGHTS network. They had to suffer through pilot masterclass programmes that combined the inner game with work and mentoring practice. Some stuff worked – some did not. They were open to providing feedback and letting me know their thoughts. *Agile by Choice*, by and large, is the result of these many trial-and-error workshops held over past years. Thank you for your patience. In that sense, *Agile by Choice* is dedicated to you.

My final thanks are for my wife, Charleen. She has supported my work on digging deeper into the inner game, and now she has taken her own route into deep Ayurveda. It's my time to return to some household duties. I am anxious to learn when *Agile by Choice* and her paths will cross or merge to create something new that we have not seen yet.

Lukas Michel
St Moritz, February 2021

FOREWORD

Working with executives from around the globe, I observe certain recurring themes and have come to understand that one of the most pressing and challenging issues confronting business executives is dealing with the accelerated rate of change. Finding ways to adapt to rapid changes in customer preferences, technology, demographics, employee perceptions about work, governmental oversight, global and local economics, and so much more is what keeps many business leaders up at night. With a great variety of books on the subject and consultants who promote their version of a change process, the questions for most executives are 'Where to begin?' and 'What will work quickly (because I have to report to the board of directors in three months)?' Yes, it is widely known that the vast majority of change initiatives fail to deliver satisfactory results. Some research shows the failure rate to be as high as 80%, so the reasonable question becomes, 'Why begin a process that has a low probability of succeeding?' The answer is, 'Because we must, otherwise...'

Lukas Michel's fourth book, *Agile by Choice*, builds and expands on his novel model and diagnostic approach first described in *The Performance Triangle: Diagnostic Mentoring to Manage Organizations and People for Superior Performance in Turbulent Times. Agile by Choice* clearly illustrates how agile management differs from the widely known agile and scrum methodology for software development by focusing the reader's attention on people rather than process. Agile management proposes that organizations must be designed in a way that enables executives and people throughout the organization to make minute adaptations in response to internal or external changes rather than complex, time-consuming and costly change initiatives that are disruptive to the organization.

The migration to agile management is, in large part, a shift in mental models about the nature of work and people doing the work in an organization; it challenges much of the traditional management models that executives have been taught in MBA programmes and that worked fine in the past century. The shift in mental models towards agile management must be a conscious decision beginning at the highest executives' levels in the C-suite. *Agile by Choice* leads the reader through the multiple dimensions that make up the Performance Triangle, offering deep insight into the people-related dynamics within an organization with exercises and thought-provoking questions that help readers reach that 'Aha!' moment where they connect with their organization. For readers who have read Lukas' prior books, *Agile by Choice* offers a deeper dive into the dimension of agile management. For those who are new to agile management, *Agile by Choice* is a thought-provoking exploration of the existing mental models for managing people and encourages readers to ask whether there is a better way to design their organizations that maximizes the performance of people and, ultimately, the organization as a whole.

Prof Dr Herb Nold
Polk State College, Lakeland, Florida, USA

PREFACE

In this book, I will argue that agile starts with the leader, who personally makes the shift to people-centricity. If leaders want their organizations to become more agile, then they first need to transform themselves before they interfere to change their organizations. The shift from traditional command-and-control to enabling people is a transformation that requires experience which most leaders don't have. Just talking about agile is not the same as practising it. Without the initial personal shift and focus on people, the larger organizational shift is doomed to fail. As such, this book guides your choice of agile, supports you to personally make the shift, and offers ideas and tools to help you achieve mastery in putting agile to work in your organization. A people-centric attitude must precede your choice of agile.

Fine nuances in your language reveal where you are: "empowering people," "set targets," "we need to educate leaders," "middle managers don't get it," "people need strong leadership." If you hear yourself using these or similar phrases, then it's time to deeply dig into this book and make agile your choice.

Here is your first break. If you are not already convinced to read *Agile by Choice*, then I suggest you use Tool #1, The Virus Check. Viruses are interference that willingly or unwillingly creeps into your organization to limit the potential of your people.

The people-centric shift follows the principles of mentoring with awareness, insights and learning as the steps. As such, *Agile by Choice* functions as a workbook that raises awareness of the possibility of turning opinions into meaning, provides the insights required to separate symptoms from root causes, and guides learning so as to translate ideas into action for you to make your personal shift. The workbook will be your companion for your personal journey with breaks on the way to agile.

Throughout this book, agile breaks serve as nudges that will challenge your thinking, offer additional insights and facilitate your decisions during your agile journey. Each break contains the following components:

 Your challenges: List them – this clears your mind.

 Your insights: Write them down so you can share them.

Your decisions: Document them – you will need good reasons.

Agile by Choice expands on leadership, going beyond my three previous books, which offer different perspectives on agile and people-centric management along the following dimensions:

- *The Performance Triangle* (Michel, 2013) is a compendium on strategic agility with 9 business cases, 50 elements and 300 practices.
- *Management Design* (Michel, 2017; 2nd edition) presents visual thinking and the process of designing agile management at scale with 16 business cases.
- *People-Centric Management* (Michel, 2020) contains nine business cases and explores the transformation process required to establish people-centric management and agile organizations.

Agile by Choice adds an individual dimension to agile, people-centric and dynamic capabilities. It starts with the individual executive who wants their management and organization to transform to agile. *The Performance Triangle, Management Design, People-Centric Management* and *Agile by Choice* combine to form (respectively) a model, the thinking, the process and the action plan, together providing a holistic perspective on agile, people-centricity and dynamism that starts at the top:

- If you were born agile and lead that way, I suggest that you use *Management Design* to scale agile throughout your organization.
- If you are in charge of an organization that needs to become agile, then I suggest you read *The Performance Triangle* to dig into the elements that make up a truly agile organization. Use the diagnostic tool in that book to raise awareness.

- If you are about to start your agile transformation, *People-Centric Management* will help you to expedite the process with your management team. Use the diagnostic tool in that book to gain insights and raise awareness of people-centricity.
- If you are digital native and want to dig deeper into the agile elements, then I suggest that you use the free AGILE SCAN tool (see Agilityinsights.net) to find out what people-centric, agile and dynamic capabilities can add to your bottom line.
- If you wish to work on yourself to become agile before you begin to make changes with your management team and organization, then continue to read *Agile by Choice*. Use the Agile Diagnostic (Tool #4) to guide and expedite your learning.

Agile by Choice helps you to establish the conditions for talents to use their full potential, perform at their peak and meet higher challenges. That's what people-centricity is all about. Your personal challenges (Chapter 1) set the context; the five leadership dimensions of people, organization, management, work and operations (introduced in Chapter 2) define the work environment; the inner game (covered in Chapter 3) offers the techniques; and resources (Chapter 4) provide the means for talents like you to perform at the peak. The inner game constitutes the art of relaxing distorting thoughts. It is a technique for coping with higher challenges. Doubts, stress, fear, biased focus, and limiting concepts and assumptions distort our thoughts, decisions, behaviours and actions. This keeps us from operating at our full potential. The inner game, a concept initially developed by Timothy Gallwey (2000), the author of the renowned *Inner Game* books on tennis, golf and work, provides essential insights into what is required for people to learn faster and perform at their peak.

A full overview of this book is as follows:
- Chapter 1 is Nudge #1 on your agile journey. It helps you to examine your business challenges and establish a solid foundation from which to start the agile journey. It offers the *why* for agile.
- Chapter 2 raises your awareness of agile around five leadership dimensions: people, organization, management, work and operations. It offers the Agile Diagnostic tool with models

to point to the elements that require your attention. As such, Nudge #2 offers the *what* of agile.

- Chapter 3 explores the power of the inner game and flow with awareness, choice and trust as the key elements of people-centric and agile work. Nudges #3 to #6 are about the *how* of agile and about enabling you to reach clarity of flow.
- Chapter 4 examines your resources: how you can use energy, focus of attention, time and space to ensure sufficient resources are available for you to make the people-centric shift. Nudges #7 to #11 mobilize your resources to make agile work.
- Chapter 5 is about decision-making – the opportunity to establish leadership everywhere. Nudge #12 takes you through what executives do and the need for agile systems.
- Chapter 6 explains the shift to people-centricity and how this unlocks your talents and those of your people. Nudge #13 is about how your mind-shift will make you the leader.
- Chapter 7 suggests that you engage your team in the agile experience. Nudge #14 offers awareness and insights around your experiential learning.

Agile by Choice comes with an appendix of 21 tools. I have used many of them over the past 35 years with executives all over the world. I am thankful to my many expert colleagues, from whom I have borrowed some of the templates, ideas and practices. They are now yours.

Here are the beginnings of seven stories (based on real-life companies) that illustrate the journey of seven executives who have made the choice of agile.

The chief executive: entrepreneurship. He is the new CEO of a large insurance company with 35,000 employees across the world. Bureaucracy has been creeping into the culture, driven by many staff experts with the best intentions to make the company better, and this bureaucracy is keeping highly trained executives from caring about the needs of demanding clients. The idea is to bring back entrepreneurship in a company that was once known as an innovative industry leader. The task is to gather all support staff around a shared agile agenda.

The manager: innovation. He is a new business executive in charge of a division of a large pharmaceutical company with 2,500 employees in locations across the US, Europe and Japan. Agile is his choice but his management team is stuck in tradition. The question is how to get there faster, reinstall innovation and gain traction with a strong product pipeline. The task is to initiate agile with the management team.

The architect: agile management. He is the chief of staff of a Swiss-based global think-tank with the challenge of matching the current business model with a management model that retains a high degree of flexibility in its operation. With a dominant annual event, the challenge is to maintain a level of staff capable of shaping the agenda and delivering a superior event. The task is to engage the executive team in the conversation, encouraging its members to serve as architects of agility.

The translator: CEO office. She is the CEO office manager of a South African food company with 250 employees. Her challenge is to introduce agile in an environment that requires a high level of quality and total control throughout the entire value chain. Agile is on the other scale with an executive team and managers that do not know any different. The task is to translate between agile aspirations and management reality.

The integrator: culture. He is the manager of a mid-sized US city with the vision to establish the best city administration in the country. With nearly 2,500 employees and 150 managers and supervisors in 12 departments that range from IT to the airport to police and gardening, he has a difficult integration task with a culture that serves as the umbrella. The task is to get all managers involved in a process that will make the city more agile and service friendly.

The chair: growth. He is the investor, founder and chair of a sugar manufacturing start-up in the Middle East. His challenge is to scale agile management in line with business growth. With new managers and staff frequently joining the company to enable it to cope with this growth, agile is needed to manage the company's development. The task is to create a scale model that can support the growth.

The executive coach: engagement. She is one of those executive coach who can handle big leaders with big transformation challenges. Her challenge is that most of her clients need agile, but few recognize the need and even fewer know how to go about it. Dominant leaders want change in their organizations. The task is to get the process started with these leaders to prevent other fruitless change projects in their organizations.

Agile by Choice guides your personal shift with 14 nudges. They are gentle pushes for you to take a break, think, learn and initiate your shift:

#1   Three **tools** to map your *expectations*, strategy and operating mode

#2   Five **dimensions** to explore the agile *choices* regarding organization and management

#3   Four **principles** of the *inner game* to help you reach flow more often

#4   The **light** that raises *awareness* to help you reach clarity and better cope with complexity

#5   The **strategy** of *choice* and self-responsibility to move despite ambiguity

#6   The **condition** of *trust*, which mobilizes resources in times of uncertainty

#7   The **formula** for your *return on management*

#8   The **power** of the *energy* that drives engagement but requires refuelling

#9   The **technique** to *focus attention* and learn to perform in a volatile environment

#10   The **rhythm** to use *time* efficiently

#11   The **protocol** that creates your *space* and accountability

#12   The **skills** to make *decision-making* your advantage in the knowledge era

#13   The **mindset** that will unlock the *talent* and distribute leadership everywhere

#14   The **cycle** of *experiential learning* to establish new experience with leadership everywhere through agile capabilities, a client focus, people-centric management and value for society

Agile by Choice offers experiential support with tools and exercises to enable leaders to personally gain experience with agile, learn fast to experience its benefits, and use the experience they have gained to personally make the shift to the principles of the inner game and use resources and better decision-making to reach agile mastery in today's world.

CHAPTER 1

Business Challenges

This chapter offers Nudge #1 on your agile journey. It examines your business challenges and establishes the foundation from which to start your agile journey. The opening section, 'My Self,' offers you the opportunity to create the map of your personal challenges and compare them with your investment in resources. This initiates your personal agile journey.

Expectations establish clarity about your destination. They collate the past, the present and the future. Expectations frame the intent of your agile journey. Next, clarity on your organization's strategy sets the direction of your agile journey as a choice that determines your dominant business model. Your business determines your dominant operating mode. It's a choice between traditional and agile ways of doing things. To make this choice, we need to introduce a schism to split the executive into leadership (the individual) and systems (the institution).

The leadership part offers the reasons why it makes sense for you to use *Agile by Choice* and start the journey by making the shift to people-centricity yourself.

NUDGE #1: MAP YOUR CHALLENGES
Use expectations, strategy and operating modes to initiate your thinking about your choice of agile.

Now, start with yourself.

MY SELF

Let's start with yourself and the challenges that wake you up at 3am. The processes outlined in this section creates the map of your challenges and contrasts them with your resources. Knowing yourself initiates your personal agile journey. It sets the stage.

In order to tackle complex, dynamic challenges with uncertainties, leaders must expand their skills to combine old and new information. Three approaches help you stretch your thinking:

- **Application**: relate the unknown with the known. This is the kind of thinking where known procedures and methods of planning and implementation are used to deliver results quickly. Solutions are found by activating past experiences.
- **Expertise**: gain deep insights on a specific issue. People with knowledge of a topic contribute when the question is new or when existing methods cannot help to address the issue. Experts add new insights and analytical diagnostics. This results in solutions that perfectly fit the specific situation and context.
- **Origination**: find new solutions through new thinking. This is the kind of integrated and comprehensive thinking that expands horizons. Double-loop learning (Argyris, 1991) and systems thinking (Senge, 1990) often help. Assumptions are questions and usual responses are tested. The idea is to gain further insights on complex issues. As such, new solutions emerge.

When reality hits the plan, then it's time to take your Challenge Break and think. Use Tool #2, My Challenge Map, in combination with Tool #3, Take a Break, to get you started.

Your Challenge Break will help you to identify your most pressing challenges and identify ways to effectively address them.

As you continue reading *Agile by Choice*, you will likely come back to your challenges. The challenge map will guide your shift to people-centricity on your way to agile.

MY CHALLENGE BREAK

Identify your business challenges using the following steps:

 What are your challenges? Use Tool #2, My Challenge Map

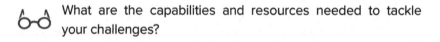 What are the capabilities and resources needed to tackle your challenges?

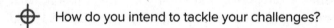 How do you intend to tackle your challenges?

EXPECTATIONS

Expectations determine your destination. They clarify your intent and frame your agile journey. This is about collapsing the past, the present and the future into the now.

We all want to succeed in what we do. Organizations search for additional growth. But "growth is the scoreboard, not the game" (Hamel, 1998). We want to lower transaction costs, but every additional perfection adds to cost. We want more performance, less risk. But more control leads to the opposite. We feel as if we are losing control. As individuals, we search for joy, serendipity, performance and flow. We stretch our limits and take more risks. We use our existing skills to tackle new challenges when new skills are needed. Both organizations and individuals face the challenges of a more demanding outer game, a game that requires new capabilities and skills. The outer game represents all decisions, challenges, interferences, opportunities and goals that you and your organization expect to encounter on your path from the present to the future destination.

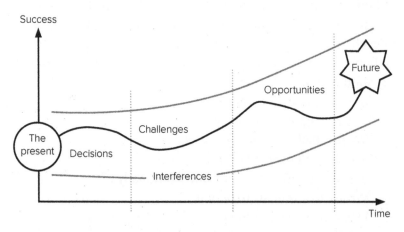

FIGURE 1: EXPECTATIONS

Against popular belief, the path to success is never a straight line. We know from the path effect in physics that development is usually not the result of a plan rather a combination of all possible paths. Reality hits plans when challenges change, interference keeps you from exploiting your potential, and new opportunities require decisions to change. Expectations about the future (Figure 1) must include the idea that capabilities must fit challenges, capturing opportunities needs the right timing, and interference will limit potential. With the many unknowns, it is most likely that your plans will follow the course of a roller coaster. Sometimes they will perform better, and sometimes worse.

Where do we start from? To begin our journey, we need a clear picture from which to start. Awareness with a sense of reality helps us to gain a deep understanding of our current reality. Performance happens in the present. Collapsing the past, the present and the future into the now can be called 'past-present-future.' When all three are seen at once, flow occurs and performance matches our potential.

Second-order management, the indirect, observing and consultative approach to getting things done, states that leaders need to create reality in order to behave in a goal-oriented manner. The task of management is to replace the control of the uncontrollable with mobilizing to construct the future. Once reality has been decided, the task is to act as if this is reality (first-order management). It is about observing people change and adapt to the new reality. Hence, the quality of management is the key to current performance and the development of the company.

When you hear any of the following from your team, you definitely should make a choice:

- "It is only an execution issue..."
- "It is an alignment problem..."
- "We just have to be more focused..."
- "It's the fault of regulation..."
- "Our competitors are behaving irrationally..."
- "We are in a transition period..."
- "Everyone's losing money..."
- "Asia/Latin America went bad..."

- "We are investing for the long term..."
- "Investors don't understand our strategy..."

Making excuses is not the same as making a choice. The Expectation Break below will help you to identify your expectations and make your choice.

MY EXPECTATION BREAK

 What should your ambitions be? What do you expect your business to look like in ten years?

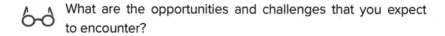 What are the opportunities and challenges that you expect to encounter?

 How do you expect to get to your destination quickly?

STRATEGY

The next break on your agile journey is your organization's strategy. Clarity on strategy guides your business model to set the direction of your agile journey.

POSITIONING

The strategy determines your business and operating models, which mark the starting point of every agile journey. Hax and Majluf (1996) suggest nine distinct strategies that cover most businesses, whether start-ups, traditional organizations, platforms or ecosystems of networked companies. The choices are presented in a table that aligns the positioning with a company's core processes. Figure 2 offers a choice of nine different business strategies to help you decide on your dominant strategy.

Process \ Positioning	Product	Customer	System	
Operation	Product performance	Customer benefits	System performance	Lowest cost and asset use, best quality
Customer	Distribution channels	Customer bundles	Unique system	Understanding of customer needs
Innovation	Product innovation	Service innovation	Architecture innovation	Newest thing on the market
	Best product (Lowest price or highest quality)	Specific client solution	Different business model and system	

FIGURE 2: BUSINESS STRATEGY

The best product performance builds on traditional form of competition. Customers are attracted through low cost or due to differentiation that introduces new features. Innovation is centred on internal product development. The total customer solution strategy is the complete reversal of the best product approach. Instead of commoditizing the customer, a deep understanding of the customer and the relationship are created. An integrated supply chain links key suppliers and customers. Innovation is aimed at the joint development of distinctive products. The systems strategy includes the extended enterprise, with customers, suppliers and complementors as a network, a platform or an ecosystem that may span the entire value chain from product to delivery. Distribution channels are a key consideration as they involve ownership or restricting access.

Aligning the key activities with the three strategies follow three adaptive processes: operational effectiveness, customer targeting and innovation. Operations is about the manufacturing and delivery of products and services. It aims for the most effective use of assets, such as machines and infrastructure, to support the chosen strategic position of the company. Customer targeting is about the management of the customer interface. It should establish the best revenue infrastructure of the company. Innovation is about new product development. It should ensure a continuous stream of new products and services to maintain the future viability of the business.

BUSINESS MODEL

With clarity on your strategy, you now can determine your dominant business model: exploitation business models concern choice, efficiency and selection, whereas exploration is about search, variation and innovation.

- **Exploitation model**: In line with James G. March (1991), "exploitation includes such things as refinement, choice, production, efficiency, selection, implementation, execution." Exploitation consists of the refinement of existing technology, requiring individual coordination (Nooteboom, 1999).

- **Exploration model**: As March (1991) further states, "exploration includes things captured by terms such as search, variation, risk taking, experimentation, play, flexibility, discovery, innovation." Exploration is an adaptable and flexible process, which has to adapt itself to the new configuration the company can discover and arises from individual deviance as a source of innovation (Nooteboom, 1999).
- **Hybrid model**: Combining exploitation and exploration poses a dilemma as they compete for the same scarce resources. The challenge is to combine both in a way that guarantees the survival of the company – a trade-off between variation and selection, between change and stability. The combination means learning as the concurrent development and diffusion of knowledge in the organization.

Operational effectiveness is all about exploitation, whereas innovation relates to exploration. The hybrid model combines both exploitation and exploration. Your Strategy Break will help you to determine your strategy and select your business model.

MY CHALLENGE BREAK

 What is your current dominant business strategy, and what will your dominant strategy be in the future?

What is your current dominant business model, and what will your dominant business model be in the future?

Remember, strategy and business models must match.

 Do your current and future strategies and business models differ?

In deciding whether your current and future strategies and models differ, use judgement and good decision-making.

- Information is always incomplete
- There is never enough time, and it is always the wrong time
- Decisions are always difficult
- Difficult decisions arise from the lack of clarity
- Decisions always include uncertainty and risks

 What change(s) in your strategy and business model do you anticipate or make?

OPERATING MODES

The operating mode of your business determines your dominant operating system. That's your next decision on your agile journey. It's a choice between traditional management, on the one hand, and people-centric and dynamic ways of doing things, on the other.

This choice is essential as it determines how your organization operates, competes and collaborates. People-centricity and dynamism are two individual, organizational and managerial capabilities that are essential for success in today's world.

Today, leaders face a business environment that differs in many aspects from that of the past. It's a dynamic context with increasing volatility, uncertainty, complexity and ambiguity (VUCA).[1] In our research (Michel, Anzengruber, Wölfle and Hixson, 2018), my colleagues and I have identified digitalization and the changing nature of work as triggering the need for people-centric and dynamic responses. Digitalization reduces information search costs and reinforces the dynamics of the changes in the external and internal environments. The changed nature of work demands people-centric capabilities where distributed knowledge and leadership can be effectively applied. Changes in the degree of external challenges expedite the shift from a stable to a dynamic system. The distribution of knowledge and leadership shift management from a traditional to a people-centric mode.

Agile is a choice that is distinct from traditional ways of getting things done (Figure 3). Those ways worked well in a stable context but fail in the new, dynamic context.

The traditional 'plan-do-check-act' approach is in trouble:

- **Plan**: volatility shortens cycles
- **Do**: command fails to reduce complexity
- **Check**: trust beats control amid uncertainty
- **Act**: standard operating procedures fail in an ambiguous context

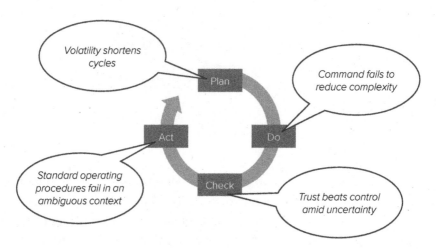

FIGURE 3: TRADITIONAL MANAGEMENT

The new context (Figure 4) distinguishes between traditional and agile. Traditional works well in a stable environment where knowledge is concentrated at the top. Agile is needed to operate in a dynamic context where knowledge is distributed, with people-centric leadership everywhere.

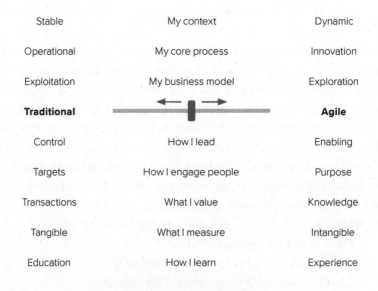

Stable	My context	Dynamic
Operational	My core process	Innovation
Exploitation	My business model	Exploration
Traditional		**Agile**
Control	How I lead	Enabling
Targets	How I engage people	Purpose
Transactions	What I value	Knowledge
Tangible	What I measure	Intangible
Education	How I learn	Experience

FIGURE 4: THE NEW CONTEXT

The dominant context determines your business's core process, and the business model indicates where you stand between the traditional and the agile operating modes. Clarity on your operating mode gives way to identifying your dominant management model.

But before we do that, we need one more stop: think about yourself and your organization. Today's work requires collaboration and cooperation. As most work involves more than one person, we need to expand our view beyond the executive. To continue the conversation about agile and discuss operating modes, we need to introduce a schism: a critical junction that splits the executive into leadership (the individual) and systems (the institution).

Executives do not operate in isolation. They work with their management teams, lead people and need to worry about the functioning of their organization. While 'work *in* the system' is the focus of this book, we cannot talk about executive effectiveness without a glance at 'work *on* the system' and the elements of agility. Figure 5 splits the idea of a single executive into the individual and the institution.

The Individual: Leadership	The Institution: Systems
The glass is half full or half empty	The glass may need to be twice as big
Work *in* the system	Work *on* the system
People development	Dynamic systems development
Heroic view: leaders as heroes	Post-heroic view: collective minds
Hard: can hardly be changed	Soft: can be changed (contrary to popular belief)
Source of people-centric thinking	The condition that creates the opportunity

FIGURE 5: THE INDIVIDUAL AND THE INSTITUTION

This schism helps us further dig into the sources of people-centric thinking, while at the same time talking about the conditions required to apply good leadership. As an executive, you have the duty and right (accountability) to shape your conditions and those of every individual in your organization.

But beware: in conflict, the institution always wins. System defects are always personalized. The dramaturgy of failure is always the same. Step 1: people note an institutional interference or error (the 'what is'). Then, step 2 kicks in. The error falls back on the individual (this is the 'what should be'). That's why you should simultaneously care about leadership and systems.

Figure 6 introduces leadership and systems in their contextual setting: traditional, dynamic and people-centric operating modes. The combination of means (systems) and ends (people, leadership) leads to four operating modes: control, engagement, change and enabling.

FIGURE 6: FOUR OPERATING MODES

- **Control**: In a stable environment where knowledge is concentrated at the top, traditional management and institutional control dominate. The thinking and doing are separated, which justifies traditional, bureaucratic control. Traditional management applies direct control through narrow targets. Interactions focus on disseminating strategy and ruling performance. Decisions are made by leaders and narrow targets maintain the focus to keep people on track.

- **Engagement**: In a knowledge-driven environment with little change, the engagement mode dominates. People (the ends) are tightly controlled by traditional means. People-centric leadership supports self-responsible people guided by broad direction. Management aligns individual interests through visions, beliefs, boundaries and values. As Simons (1995) articulates, "in the absence of management action, self-interested behaviour at the expense of organizational goals is inevitable." Self-responsibility and broad direction are balanced with hierarchical power and institutional bureaucracy.
- **Change**: In a dynamic market environment with centralized decision-making, direct intervention through change dominates. Dynamic systems (the means) meet traditional ways to lead people (the ends). Change modes operate through a market control setting where managers alter the resource base, align interests through incentives and restructure accountabilities in response to market changes.
- **Enabling**: In a dynamic context with knowledge distributed throughout the organization, the enabling mode dominates. People-centric leadership (the ends) and dynamic systems (the means) match. Traditional rules-based management approaches are not effective. Under these conditions, enabling modes support fast decision-making and proactive, flexible action, which together lead to robust outcomes.

Business models and operating modes must match. Exploitation business models favour control approaches. Exploration business models demand enabling management. Hybrid business models often use change or engagement modes.

Your dominant business model determines your operating mode and your dominant management model. Your choice of management model has deep implications for your leadership, organization and management.

The change from your current to your future management model can be called the people-centric shift. The ideas in this chapter will determine your dominant operating mode and your current and future management models.

Before you make up your mind about which mode works best for you, it's time to take a break and carry out the Agile Diagnostic. To do this, work through the questions and guidance in Tool #4 in the appendix.

The diagnostic questions will raise your awareness of the critical dimensions of leadership with its people-centric, agile and dynamic capability elements. They will help you to determine your current capabilities, and this information will feed into your conversation about your people-centric shift.

Using the results of the Agile Diagnostic, the Operating Mode Break will help you to make your choices about your dominant operating mode and management model.

MY OPERATING MODE BREAK

 What is your current dominant operating mode, and what will your dominant operating mode be in the future?

What is your current dominant management model, and what will your dominant management model be in the future?

Remember, business models and operating modes must match. Using the results of questions 17–20 in the Agile Diagnostic (Tool #4), plot your current status on the chart below. This will give you your dominant operating mode.

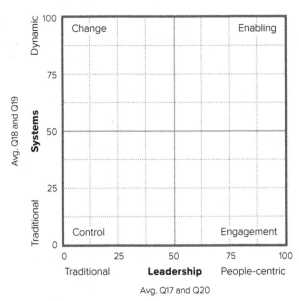

 Do your current and future management models differ?

 What is the people-centric shift that you anticipate?

SUCCESS

Does your leadership matter? This is more than a rhetorical question. Does good leadership make a difference when it comes to success, results, performance and flow? The instant response is yes – otherwise, why would we engage in developing good leadership practices? But, although there are lots of good anecdotal examples, it is hard to find substantial evidence of a direct impact of leadership on outcomes. That being said, there is substantial literature that explains specific aspects of leadership and their contributions. Figure 7 shows a simple overview of the relevant factors. The purpose of this overview is to make the case that leadership, systems and culture – the three parts of the Performance Triangle (see Michel, 2013) – explain the things that can be managed and influenced.

Success = *f* (leadership, systems, culture, opportunities and risks, serendipity)

FIGURE 7: DETERMINANTS OF SUCCESS

Leadership, systems and culture are discretionary factors that require management decisions. They can be managed and therefore can make a difference. Opportunities and risks depend on endogenous factors but also require decisions. They are the challenges that you accept. Parts of these factors depend on the quality of leadership. This leaves us with serendipity, which is outside our control.

The use of appropriate interaction mechanisms determines how decisions are made. They depend on the leader's skills and the quality of the supporting systems. The design of systems as tools, routines and rules provides choice about strategy, structure and capabilities to represent the operating constraints that explain important aspects of success. All these elements represent distinct executive decisions.

It is important to note that investors can diversify this unsystematic risk: the promises, innovation, reputation, talent and (missed) opportunities.

Therefore, I conclude that leaders can make a difference through actively shaping their management dimensions and elements: leadership, systems and culture. It's work *on* your organization's operating system.

This chapter separated agile from traditional ways of getting things done when knowledge matters and the context becomes dynamic. In the next chapter, Nudge #2 expands on the leadership dimensions and elements that you can shape.

MY BUSINESS CHALLENGES

A choice must be made between traditional ways of getting things done (which work well in a stable context but fail in a dynamic context) and agile including people-centric and dynamic.

KEY CHAPTER IDEAS

- Agile starts with yourself
- Your management model determines how your organization operates
- Strategy, business models and management models must match
- Your leadership matters – work *on* your system

ACTION AGENDA

- Know yourself – map out your challenges
- Clarify your expectations
- Determine your strategy and business model
- Decide on your operating mode and management model
- Diagnose agile with Tool #4 in the appendix

FURTHER READING

On strategy: Hax, A. C. and Majluf, N. D. (1996). *The Strategy Concept and Process: A Pragmatic Approach*. New York: Palgrave.

On operating modes: Michel, L., Anzengruber, J., Woelfle, M. and Hixson, N. (2018). Under what conditions do rules-based and capability-based management modes dominate? *Risks*, 6(2): 32.

On the diagnostic: Nold, H., Anzengruber, J., Michel, L. and Wölfle, M. (2018). Organizational agility: Testing validity and reliability of a diagnostic instrument. *Journal of Organizational Psychology*, 18(3): DOI 10.33423/jop.v18i3.1292.

CHAPTER 2

Five Leadership Dimensions

Agile is a choice for leadership everywhere; it involves learning, agile organization, people-centric management, customer-focused strategies and sustainable outcomes. This chapter is your second nudge to raise your awareness of agile on five dimensions. It offers insights on what truly matters with your choice of agile. In the five dimensions, people are at the centre and leadership is everywhere:

1. **People**: the inner game and learning
2. **Organization**: the elements of the agile Performance Triangle
3. **Management**: four people-centric levers
4. **Work**: the focus on clients
5. **Operations**: dynamic capabilities and outcomes

Agile maturity levels (introduced later on in the section on operations) offer a scale for you to identify where your organization stands. The canvas (see Figure 23, later in this chapter) frames the five dimensions and serves as a tool that you can use to document your agile journey. This is for your work *on* the system.

NUDGE #2: EXPLORE THE DIMENSIONS
Use the people, organization, management, work and operations dimensions to expand your thinking and choice of agile.

Start now with the individual people dimension. Use your results from the Agile Diagnostic (Tool #4) together with the visuals to distil your organization's agile capabilities and document your assumptions, the potential, the interference, gaps, key issues and initiatives with the canvas (Figure 23 and Tool #6, Document Agile).

#1 PEOPLE

The people dimension (Figure 8) is about the individual as a leader or employee. It is about people as executives who make decisions. They play an inner game and an outer game (Gallwey, 2000). With this, agile has the potential to distribute leadership everywhere. This section helps you to identify the principles of the inner game that are relevant to you.

To capture relevant opportunities, people must deal with the personal challenges (the inner game) and external challenges (the outer game) they have set out to tackle. This bridges the outer game with the inner game of work. In that sense, the outer game represents the internal and external challenges that people face when they perform. The bridge is needed to ensure that minimum interference occurs from within the individual and the organization. Interference limits potential and reduces overall performance.

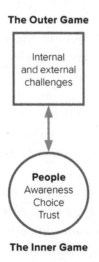

The Outer Game

Internal
and external
challenges

People
Awareness
Choice
Trust

The Inner Game

FIGURE 8: THE PEOPLE DIMENSION

New work is different. Digitalization offers new ways to work with implications for leadership, organization and management. Knowledge work, responsibility and motivation frame the playing field.

KNOWLEDGE WORK

'Knowledge work' means that people – not just leaders – have the full ability to act and make decisions. Distributed decision-making requires an agile operating environment in which people can apply their full potential. This is in sharp contrast to the traditional principles of the 'controlling mode,' where interference prevents people from using their knowledge and experience to seize opportunities. In the agile mode, the thinking and doing are united. Knowledge work is made up of five elements:

- **Understand**: Information and immediate feedback raise awareness of what is important. This helps people to understand what matters and focuses attention. Superior understanding requires that sensors are not on mute and amplifiers work properly.
- **Think**: 'Knowledge people' have a set of mental maps. It helps them to make sense of situations and make decisions. The benefits for an organization come not only from individual thinking but also from collective thinking. The thinking requires an opportunity to create meaning and asks for a deliberate choice to move in one direction.
- **Act**: This involves translating ideas into action. The task is to mobilize resources to get things done. People put their energy into things that they care about. And energy requires action to be meaningful. Contribution requires the opportunity to apply knowledge, and to support and balance freedom and constraints. Superior contributions build on the trust of people and in people.
- **Engage**: Attention is a limited resource; energy is required to maintain it at a high level. Attention must be focused to prevent distraction from competing demands. A high level of engagement requires beliefs, motives and purpose.

- **Adhere**: Energy adds pull and a positive tension to the boundaries of an organization: the stretch between safely staying within the boundaries and the search for opportunities outside the boundaries. This tension requires a balance between efficiency and entrepreneurship. A high level of adherence maintains a good balance.

Figure 9 contrasts traditional and agile approaches to knowledge work according to these five elements.

	Understand	Think	Act	Engage	Adhere
In an agile context...	Use information to get work done	Make decisions	Are motivated by a sense of purpose	Have clear priorities	Are empowered and clear about norms
people use their potential	Unlimited information	Unlimited opportunities; encouraged to take risks	Increased pressures	Limited attention; limited resources	Growing temptations for outside the boundaries
In a traditional context...	Information is limited to the top	Leaders make decisions	Leaders motivate for performance	Employees execute...	...and control what gets done
people are bound by limitations	Lack of information	Lack of opportunities; fear of risk	Lack of purpose	Conflicting goals; lack of resources	Lack of boundaries

FIGURE 9: CONTRASTING KNOWLEDGE WORK

Agile assumes a mindset where people want to contribute, develop and work in a goal-oriented way. This is in sharp contrast to traditional assumptions, where people are motivated, controlled and trained. Figure 10 illustrates the differences for employees and leaders.

Agile assumptions	Traditional assumptions
Knowledge employees...	*As compared to...*
Want to contribute	Don't do anything on their own
Want to do things right	Need to be developed
Want to achieve	Need to be directed
Want to be creative and develop	Do what they are told
Agile leaders...	*As compared to...*
Ask questions and focus	Motivate and decide; tell people what to do
Shape the environment	Judge and review
Support creativity	Sit at the top; provide instructions
Establish relationships	Are responsible, have the power to change and set the rules

FIGURE 10: ASSUMPTIONS ABOUT WORK

In an agile context, leaders have a new role: to create an environment where people can unlock their full talent.

TALENT

It's easy to say "We only hire the best talent." But who then hires the untalented people? Nobody would reasonably do that. So, what then is talent?

When we talk about talent, we assume that people have the necessary skills for peak performance. But talent is more. Talent requires beyond-average motivation and the ability to improve quickly. Both motivation and learning separate superior talent from people with the right skills. In this light, it becomes obvious that people with talent need opportunities to apply their skills and an environment where they can perform at their peak.

Motivation and learning are shared responsibilities. Self-responsibility is the source of motivation. It requires an organization that has made the choice of agile to ensure that self-responsible people can use their potential and that interference is within limits that individuals can handle. Learning also is shared between the individual and the institution. It requires the willingness to learn and the opportunity to learn. In this way, organizations that make best use of their talents make the choice of agile and offer opportunities to learn.

RESPONSIBILITY

Structure and accountability go hand in hand. Rather than redesign work, leaders should rethink their approach to delegation. Delegation means being responsible for the whole of a thing. There is no disconnect between thinking and doing. Whoever is committed and responsible in keeping promises is accountable and makes decisions.

Accountability means responsibility for someone or something, with the duty to report to someone and the agreement of shared criteria for evaluation. Self-responsibility is accountability for one's own motivation. It means choice of autonomous action, the desire to take the initiative and responding by taking creative action.

Responsibility is the number one source of motivation. You get what you put in. People accept responsibility and are accountable for results. Responsibility requires choice. It is a moral position.

Figure 11 presents the differences between accountability and responsibility. In short, managing accountability is the systemic stuff of management (systems). Creating a culture of responsibility is the stuff of leadership. Accountability cannot be given; it is assumed. It cannot be delegated. Accountability originates with the tasks that are delegated. 'Not accountable' is the mentality of clearly defined jobs, earned positions and given targets. Agile requires both accountability and responsibility.

Accountability	Responsibility
• Accountability is the liability created for the right and power to achieve results	• Responsibility is the obligation to perform a duty
• Making, keeping and managing agreements and expectations	• Feeling of ownership
• Cannot be delegated	• Can be delegated
• Cannot be shared	• Can be shared
• Outcome, solution, fulfilment	• Task, project

FIGURE 11: ACCOUNTABILITY VS. RESPONSIBILITY

MOTIVATION

Motivation is responsibility and energy; performance is the result. In most organizations, motivation is an issue because it is not well understood. Science is unclear about what motivates people to perform, but we clearly know what demotivates us. Some aspects of motivation are as follows:

- People are motivated at their own will
- Motivation is the responsibility of every human being
- Most leaders demotivate
- Group demotivation is a powerful virus (see Tool #1)
- Motivation has negative side-effects
- The motivation of employees by leaders is always late
- Systemic motivation always leads to its systemic undermining

Motivation undertaken by leaders is an action outside the control of an individual. As such, it undermines autonomy, initiative and creativity. This is why motivation requires leadership attention.

Individual performance results from a combination of readiness, capability and opportunity. Self-determination is the responsibility of the individual. The institution designs the framework for how outside control will be exerted on individuals.

WHO IS ACCOUNTABLE FOR RESPONSIBILITY AND MOTIVATION?

There are different roles when it comes to refuelling energy in organizations: individual employee responsibilities, shared accountability and institutional responsibility. Figure 12 identifies the sources of motivation as follows:

- **Readiness**: Accountability lies with the individual. Responsibility is the driving force of motivation: the intrinsic contract as a prerequisite for people getting things done. The extrinsic contract is an external-control tool that institutions use to motivate people to perform in the direction desired.
- **Capability**: There is shared accountability for capability between the individual and the institution. The organization's mechanisms for competence management define the talent's needs and offer development opportunities. But for this to be effective, individuals have to make choices about learning.
- **Opportunity**: People need to be given scope and opportunity to perform. This is the sole accountability of institutions. Leaders represent the institution and are accountable for creating a productive working environment with adequate resources, rules and processes. Creating such an environment saves considerable managerial time and puts the focus on opportunities rather than ineffective control.

Motivation	Individual Self-responsibility	Institution Outside control
Readiness: want to... Accountability lies with the individual	Responsibility, awareness, focus of attention, intrinsic contract	Purpose, extrinsic contract, awareness
Capability: able to do... Shared responsibility	Choice, skills, learning	Development, competencies
Opportunity: can do... Accountability lies with the institution	The institution offers the playing field, work, employment for the individual	Degrees of freedom (room to move), resources, process, tools (the system)

FIGURE 12: SOURCES OF MOTIVATION

Agile work relies on self-responsible people who are motivated by definition. Hence, when it comes to motivation, getting accountability and responsibility right is the key element.

THE INNER GAME

Executives play the inner game to cope with the challenges of the outer game. They make decisions: understand, think, act, engage and adhere. They accept responsibility and are accountable for their results. They source their motivation from a combination of individual responsibility and the opportunities and systems offered by the institution. Awareness, choice, trust and focus of attention constitute the inner game.

Awareness, choice and trust help people focus their attention on what counts. The result is flow – the state in which learning, performance and creativity are at their peak (Csikszentmihalyi, 1990). It shifts control to the learner and redefines the role of the leader as a coach.

Awareness involves learning by translating observed data into information without making a judgement about it. It is about having a clear understanding of the present. Non-judgemental awareness is the best way to learn. Leaders have a choice between self-confident awareness and disengagement through outside control.

Choice is the prerequisite for responsibility. It is the choice to take charge and move in the desired direction. Choice means self-determination whereas rules are determined from the outside. Leaders need to choose between choice and rules.

Trust means speed and agility. It is the cheapest leadership concept ever invented and the foundation for every business transaction. With trust, there is no need for any renegotiation of contracts when things change. Leaders have the choice between trust and mistrust or responsibility and outside control. But trust must be earned. The best way to earn trust is by delivering on promises.

Focus means self-initiated attention to what matters most. It is a conscious act of concentration that requires energy. The challenge for people is to maintain focus over a period of time. Leaders have the choice between self-initiated focus and goal achievement.

The choice of agile relies on the executive's ability to play the inner game. The inner game offers the most important principles and techniques for any individual to learn and perform. In 2000, Gallwey introduced a simple but powerful formula in *The Inner Game of Work*:

Performance = Potential - Interference

In that sense, the choice of agile must ensure that people have a work environment that is free from demotivational 'viruses,' where they can unlock their full potential and perform at their peak. Organization, the next section of this chapter, takes this on. Given the importance of the inner game, Chapters 3 to 6 are dedicated to how you can play that game well.

With clarity on knowledge work, responsibility, motivation and the inner game, you as an executive have the right and power to make the choice of agile and create a work environment based on people-centric principles. It is a choice that has the potential to distribute leadership throughout your organization. Your People Dimension Break is next.

MY PEOPLE DIMENSION BREAK

 What are your people challenges? Use your results of questions 12-15 from the Agile Diagnostic (Tool #4).

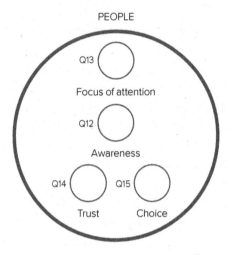

 What are the opportunities and challenges that you expect to encounter?

How do you expect to get to your destination quickly?

#2 ORGANIZATION

As an executive who has made the choice of agile and plays the inner game, it's now time for you to think about the operating environment your organization needs to succeed. In this section, you can identify your organization's operating environment, and the elements of an agile organization are the discretionary factors that require design and decisions.

But what are the elements of an agile organization? The Performance Triangle models the operating environment (Figure 13), with culture, leadership and systems at its corners and success at the top. Effective agile actions require a culture that creates shared context. Leadership is interactive to facilitate conversations around purpose, direction and performance. Systems work diagnostically, directing attention to those aspects that matter most to allow for self-directed action on deviations from the chosen path. Shared context, people's interactions and dynamic controls make up the capabilities of an agile organization. Together they help people to detect weak signals early, allow for the interpretation of that information and facilitate timely action.

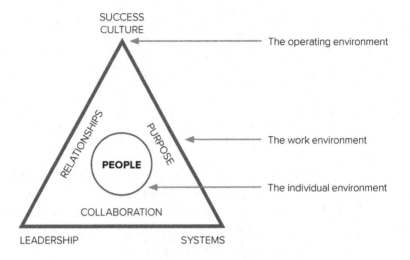

FIGURE 13: THE ORGANIZATION DIMENSION

Here are the elements of an agile organization: the Performance Triangle combines the individual environment (people dimension), the operating environment (organization dimension) and the work environment (work dimension):

- **The individual environment**: people, who engage in the inner game
- **The operating environment**: culture, leadership, systems
- **The work environment**: purpose, collaboration, relationships

The individual environment: People are at the centre of the triangle. The inner game is the means for people to perform at their peak. And it is the capability that enables speed. When people apply the inner game's principles, leaders can delegate work to the frontline of client engagement. As a result, decisions are made where the work is being done, which accelerates decisions and action. This leads to the people dimension.

The operating environment: The corners with leadership, systems and culture enable agility. Interactive leadership is about the personal interaction between leaders and employees. Dynamic systems offer the rules, routines, and tools to get work done. Culture represents the invisible guide and glue. When leaders connect and interact with employees, when systems offer guidance and feedback, when culture establishes strong bonds, then agile is at its peak.

The work environment: Purpose, relationships, and collaboration establish resilience. When people find purpose in what they are doing, when they collaborate across boundaries, and when they connect to build relationships that enhance their knowledge, then organizations can resist any external shocks. They are resilient. This leads to the stakeholder dimension.

When viruses creep into an organization, it is time for spring cleaning. These viruses might consist of toxic culture, flawed leadership or broken systems (see Tool #1 for more on viruses).

Toxic culture: Examples include faulty operating procedures, business values that are not clearly linked to outcomes, cynicism, upwards delegation, outdated reasons for centralized decision-making, a technocratic view of decision-making and a lack of shared assumptions. Culture is one of the things that gets the blame. But culture is an outcome, a feature that cannot be changed directly. A toxic culture creates subtle dissonances that are hard to detect. Fixing culture requires altering systems and leadership through workshops, mentoring and/or corporate programmes that are well crafted and orchestrated professionally. Its roots are always flawed leadership or broken systems. So, the task is to fix leadership or systems first.

Flawed leadership: Examples include excessive control, busyness, lack of time, excessive focus on detail, senselessness, excessive focus on numbers and a low amount of value added. Normally, organizations hire the best and train them to stay that way or to fit given templates. Bad leadership normally comes in counts of one – not many, otherwise we have a different problem for which there is only one fix: its entire replacement. As such, the flaw can be located and isolated as it normally resides within one person (or a small group of them). Exchanging a leader is an option but it normally comes too late. And viruses spread. An immediate reaction is evident. Fixing a leader takes time and toxins might still spread for a while. It is expensive and the likelihood of success is questionable, despite the promises of a huge 'leadership fixing industry.' Coaching or training flawed leaders is ineffective. Performance problems can be fixed where there is a will to learn. Behavioural problems (or a mixture of performance and behaviour problems) require a different choice of action.

Broken systems: Examples include bureaucratic or non-existent routines, formalism, faulty design, revisiting past decisions, slow implementation that hampers decision-making, rules infected with the 'viruses' and erroneous tools. Normally, it is a specific set of systems that cause flawed leadership. Common culprits include management by objectives, incentives, budgeting, resource allocation and communications. When any of these is broken, it affects the entire organization. Systems 'viruses' have huge leverage. Human resources, financial officers, risk officers, governance officer, and all other support officers are often the cause but not the symptom. They may be individually optimized but not aligned. Fixing systems is critical and affects the entire organization, and as such is often a risk. But not doing anything is not an option. It is comparatively cheap to fix broken systems. It is a free choice and it can be done quickly. But just fixing the toolbox might not be good enough. It might require a new design, for example to fundamentally rethink the way you lead the organization.

The symptoms of a broken toolbox are everywhere. The causes are often with the system. All of the above examples are signs of a toxic culture, missing energy or a lack of flow experiences. The result is crippled creativity and stagnation.

Now, the Organization Dimension Break will help you to explore the potentials and interference that require your attention.

MY ORGANIZATION DIMENSION BREAK

 What are your challenges? Use your results from questions 2-6 of the Agile Diagnostic (Tool #4).

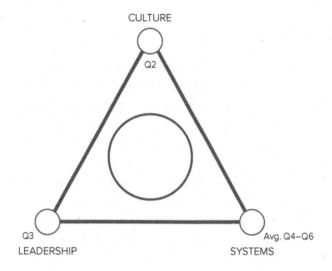

 Where is your potential, and what interference do you face?

 What are the key organizational issues that require your attention?

#3 MANAGEMENT

Now, it is time to change our perspective from the organization to the management to further explore the choice of agile. This section offers four levers that determine the dimensions of people-centric management (Figure 14). These levers translate the inner game into a management cycle. Use your results from the Agile Diagnostic (Tool #4) to identify your levers.

Business is about identifying and selecting opportunities, and transforming them into value. With people in mind, you now can use the four principles of awareness, choice, trust and attention to deliver value. Executives apply these four people-centric practices within their teams.

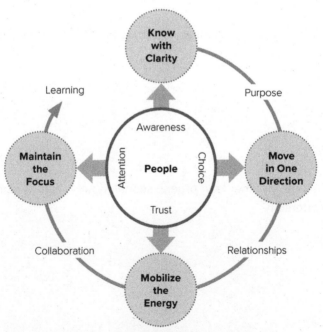

FIGURE 14: THE MANAGEMENT DIMENSION

1. **Know with clarity: raise awareness. Help people find purpose.** Motivation stems from people's self-responsibility. Purpose replaces incentives. All leaders need to do for people is to help them make sense of what truly matters. That's the best way to identify opportunities and deal with complexity in your business.

2. **Move in one direction: enable choice. Encourage relationships to enhance knowledge.** People-centric leaders delegate decisions and encourage relationships among people to enhance their skills and knowledge. Choice and direction are their means to bundle the energy to help them select the right opportunities and move in one direction as their way to deal with ambiguity.

3. **Mobilize the energy: build trust. Facilitate collaboration.** People-centric leaders facilitate self-organization based on trust as the means to deal with uncertainty. They mobilize resources in ways that enable collaboration across organizational boundaries, turning opportunities into value.

4. **Maintain the focus: focus attention.** Enable learning. People-centric leaders use beliefs and boundaries to maintain the focus of attention on what truly matters. They know that focus enables learning as the means to unlock creativity and the means to stick with chosen opportunities despite the distractions of higher volatility.

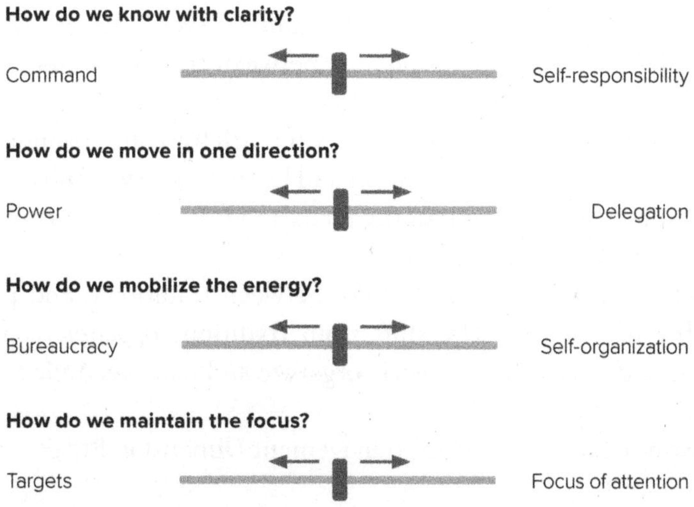

How do we know with clarity?

Command ← | → Self-responsibility

How do we move in one direction?

Power ← | → Delegation

How do we mobilize the energy?

Bureaucracy ← | → Self-organization

How do we maintain the focus?

Targets ← | → Focus of attention

FIGURE 15: FOUR PEOPLE-CENTRIC LEVERS

The four people-centric levers (Figure 15) offer a choice between traditional and people-centric management:

1. How do we know with clarity?
2. How do we move in one direction?
3. How do we mobilize the energy?
4. How do we maintain the focus?

Traditional management favours command, power, bureaucracy, and narrow targets. People-centricity is about self-responsibility, delegation, self-organization, and focus of attention. It requires a shift from left to right, from tradition to people-centricity.

Know with clarity identifies opportunities. It represents the ability to raise awareness, understand and find purpose despite complexity. Lever 1 identifies how we help people to understand and find purpose between traditional command styles and being agile through self-responsibility.

Move in one direction is the ability to select valuable opportunities. Choice requires the alignment of forces and connecting people around purpose and direction despite ambiguity. Lever 2 identifies how people align to form teams between applying traditional power and delegation.

Mobilize the energy refers to how we turn opportunities into value. It is the ability to trust our own resources and those around us, and to get things done despite uncertainty. Lever 3 identifies how we mobilize the energy to collaborate between traditional bureaucracy and self-organization.

Maintain the focus is about sticking with the chosen opportunity. It is the ability to focus attention and learn despite volatility. Lever 4 identifies how we maintain the focus and learn between traditional target-setting and attention.

The four levers offer a choice between traditional and people-centric capabilities. The shift from tradition to people-centricity means a different way to work, organize and manage. Agile requires people-centricity.

Now, take time for your Management Dimension Break.

MY MANAGEMENT DIMENSION BREAK

 What are your management challenges?
Use your results from questions 17-20 of the Agile Diagnostic
(Tool #4).

How do we know with clarity?

	0	25	50	75	100	
Command						Self-responsibility

How do we move in one direction?

	0	25	50	75	100	
Power						Delegation

How do we mobilize the energy?

	0	25	50	75	100	
Bureaucracy						Self-organization

How do we maintain the focus?

	0	25	50	75	100	
Targets						Focus of attention

 Where is your potential, and what interference do you face?

 What are your people-centric levers?

#4 WORK

This dimension connects the needs and contributions of stakeholders with the work environment. This section identifies the critical elements that determine how work is done.

Stakeholders come with their expectations about what they want from the organization and what they are willing to offer. These expectations are an important source of your organization's goals. And goals have an impact on your work environment. They may offer joy, performance and learning objectives for your inner game. Goals relating to joy offer purpose. Goals relating to performance must enable collaboration. Goals relating to learning connect people.

STAKEHOLDER EXPECTATIONS

Stakeholders have expectations of organizations: investors want returns, clients expect quality products and employees expect employment. At the same time, stakeholders provide organizations with resources: investors provide capital, clients generate profit, and employees offer hands and hearts. Value creation in every organization requires balance – the best match between stakeholder needs and their contributions to the organization. In reverse, stakeholders provide the resources that the organization needs to conduct business. Stakeholders' expectations (Figure 16) are the source of purpose, relationships and cooperation, and they are the starting point for articulating organizational goals.

Stakeholder	Needs	Contributions
Employees	Purpose, care, skills and pay	Hands, hearts, minds and voices
Customers	Fast, right, cheap and easy	Profit, growth, opinion and trust
Investors	Returns, rewards, numbers and faith	Capital, credit, risk and support
Suppliers	Profit, growth, opinion and trust	Fast, right, cheap and easy
Supervisors	Legality, fairness, safety and truth	Rules, reasons, clarity and advice
Communities	Jobs, fidelity, integrity and wealth	Image, skills, suppliers and support

FIGURE 16: STAKEHOLDER EXPECTATIONS

Employees: People come first. They are involved in enacting strategy. While technology can help to improve productivity, it cannot replace the knowledge and skills of people. People represent the collective intellectual capital with knowledge, skills, abilities and motives – scarce resources in most organizations.

Customers: Without customers there is no business; work, without a customer, is not work. This is why customers are the inspiration for employees to do a good job. Customers want high levels of 'fast, right, cheap and easy.' In return, the organization wants customers to trust it, to share information and to allow it to achieve profitable growth. Labelling everyone a customer distorts the purpose of any organization. The choice of primary customer is the person or group the organization is designed to serve. It is important to limit that choice to those constituents that transact with the organization through markets.

Investors: Are they more important than customers? This is a frequently heard, but pointless, debate. It is more important to align values with your choice of 'primary customer.' Profit is a necessary condition for the existence of a (for-profit) business and not a means in itself.

Suppliers: Just about every organization has one or more suppliers. The nature of the relationship the organization has with its suppliers is the reverse of the one it has with its clients. Decisions regarding suppliers are strategic and should not be left solely to the purchasing department.

Supervisors and community: All organizations are subject to regulatory requirements. Regulators and the public are important stakeholders that influence the decisions and behaviours of managers. Pressure groups increasingly influence public opinion, with an effect on reputation.

THE WORK ENVIRONMENT

Collaboration, purpose and relationships represent the three sides of the Performance Triangle (see Figure 13). Their configuration for the enabling operating mode (see Figure 6) sets the stage for a resilient organization with the potential to grow from within.

Purpose connects systems and cultures to people. But "there is no administrative production of purpose," in the words of Jürgen Habermas (1988). What we often hear when the climate changes is: when we lost sight of the purpose of our work, we started a discussion on motivation. When people experience their work as meaningful, they contribute with greater energy; they are physically, mentally and emotionally fully present. Purpose is created individually, subjectively. It is always 'me' that provides purpose to the world. It is called 'sense-making' not 'sense-giving.' Purpose cannot be delivered. It needs to be found or 'produced' individually.

Relationships are the cornerstones of every business transaction. In individualized people-to-people business relationships with external stakeholders, trust and agreement between employees and the organization are essential. As such, 'relationship capital' is essential to the value of a company. But good relationships come at a price. They impose a challenge on every leader of an organization. Relationships also relate to connectivity. The greater the number of connections among people in an organization, the more restrictions and boundaries they place on one another. This limits their freedom of movement and their ability to perform (Stacey, 2000).

As a result, relationships and connectivity must be tuned to the optimum level.

Collaboration is an issue because of complexity, which increases with size. We keep adding functions, geographies, departments, services, client groups and other structures to our organizations. In a complex and networked world, where knowledge matters, collaboration is more important than ever. Every structure creates barriers between people who need to work together, such as limited or distorted information flows. In addition, there is a need to resolve the very fundamental cooperation problem of employees and organizations having different, often conflicting, goals.

Now, use your Work Dimension Break to identify your elements. You may want to make a detour and first identify your stakeholder expectations with Tool #5, Review Stakeholders.

MY WORK DIMENSION BREAK

 What are your challenges? Use your results from questions 7–9 of the Agile Diagnostic (Tool #4).

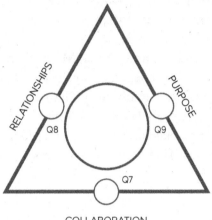

COLLABORATION

 Where is your potential, and what interference do you face?

 What are your gaps and what strategies will help you to close the gaps?

STRATEGIES FOR DEEP MEANING

Meaning offers purpose. Meaning comes from systems with explicit beliefs and boundaries (vision, mission, offering and goals) and a culture with implicit values and standards that help people find purpose, raise awareness, be motivated, be creative and unlock their talents. With purpose, they identify opportunities, stick with them, and deal with complexity and volatility. Four purpose modes (Figure 17) can be used to identify the nature of meaning in your organization.

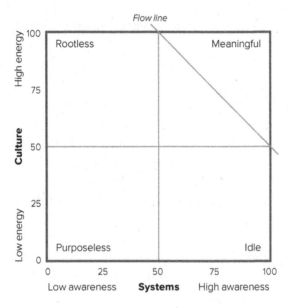

FIGURE 17: PURPOSE MODES

Meaningful purpose: high awareness, high energy. People find purpose in what they do.
- People are motivated, convinced, creative and contribute
- Awareness, accountability and self-determination prevail
- Vision, values and direction provide meaning

Idle purpose: high awareness, low energy. The lack of energy kills motivation.
- People and teams are exhausted and constantly destroy energy
- Defensive reactions prevail and are part of the culture
- Risk and boundaries dominate decisions and actions

Rootless purpose: low awareness, high energy. Headless change reigns.
- Being busy and productivity are often mixed up; action dominates
- Intensity of work is often ineffective and needs ongoing justification
- Themes and initiatives keep changing and ignore reality

Purposeless meaning: low awareness, low energy. Demotivation draws on energy.
- People are demotivated, have no choice and are busy all the time
- They lack resources, routine work dominates and complexity takes over
- Initiatives are blocked and direction is confusing

Strategies for reaching the flow line (in Figure 17) with purpose include knowing with clarity, raising awareness and helping people to find purpose. The solution involves the following:
- **Build awareness and nurture a productive culture**: Use agile systems with vision, values, strategy and routines to reduce complexity, and tools that can handle volatility.
- **Remove interference**: Fix erroneous systems and then marshal leaders to help people find purpose. The fix is systems with agile features.

Take a Purpose Break to review what you can do about meaning.

MY PURPOSE BREAK

 What are your challenges? Use your results from questions 2 and 4–6 from the Agile Diagnostic (Tool #4).

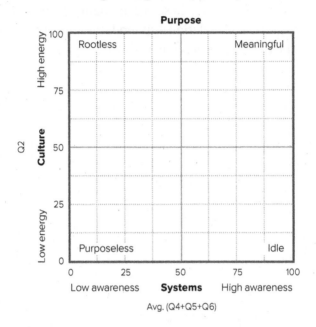

 How will you get to the flow line? Where is your potential, and what interference do you face?

What are your gaps and what strategies will help you to close the gaps?

STRATEGIES FOR STRONG CONNECTIVITY

Connectivity facilitates relationships. It comes from leadership: interactions and a culture that support people with direction, offer choice, delegate authority, use and grow knowledge, and learn. Remember, knowledge is the only resource that grows with use. Connectivity helps people to select the right opportunities and deal with ambiguity. Four relationship modes (Figure 18) can be used to identify the nature of connectivity in your organization.

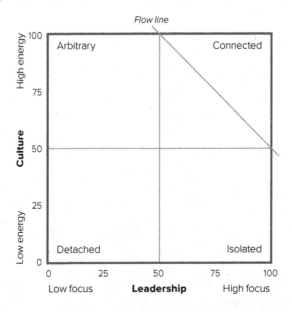

FIGURE 18: RELATIONSHIPS MODES

Connected relationships: high focus, high energy. Creative people with choice build knowledge.
- Employees have choice in how to do things
- They get the right things done
- Leaders interact, offer clarity and support the learning

Isolated relationships: high focus, low energy. Leaders keep people busy.
- Employees use up resources with long hours
- There is no capacity for anything else
- Teams work on projects in the dark with little impact

Arbitrary relationships: low focus, high energy. People are busy with scattered initiatives.
- People are always busy and need ongoing motivation
- Teams miss opportunities or the right time
- Leaders are blind to inefficiencies

Detached relationships: low focus, low energy. People are isolated and mediocrity prevails.
- People stand in each other's way for no reason
- Teams resist change and are mobilized by others
- It is hard to escape the negative spiral

Strategies for reaching the flow line and build reliable relationships include moving in one direction, enabling choice and building relationships between people so as to enhance knowledge. The solution involves the following:
- **Strengthen the focus and energize the culture**: Use agile systems (build for creativity and innovation) and rethink the culture (desired behaviours, decisions and actions).
- **Remove interference**: Fix erroneous systems, remove viruses from the culture (see Tool #1 for more on viruses) and vaccinate the culture against new viruses.

Take the Relationship Break on the next page to review what you can do about connectivity.

MY RELATIONSHIP BREAK

 What are your challenges? Use your results from the Agile Diagnostic (Tool #4).

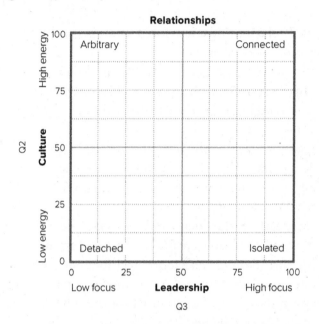

 How will you get to the flow line? Where is your potential, and what interference do you face?

What are your gaps and what strategies will help you to close the gaps?

STRATEGIES FOR EFFECTIVE COOPERATION

Cooperation enhances collaboration. Cooperation comes from systems (rules, routines and tools) and leaders (who connect people) that facilitate collaboration. Trust helps to mobilize resources and turn opportunities into value despite uncertainty. Four collaboration modes (Figure 19) can be used to identify the nature of cooperation in organizations.

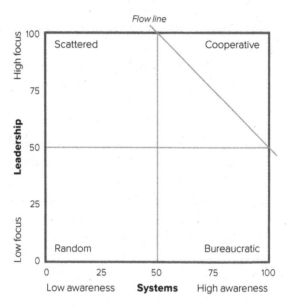

FIGURE 19: COLLABORATION MODES

Cooperative collaboration: high awareness, high focus. Trust mobilizes people and resources.
- People connect to share and collaborate with others
- Teams address important themes in the right way
- Leaders provide resources and trust teams

Bureaucratic collaboration: high awareness, low focus. Systems are in control.
- People need to navigate around bureaucracy to get things done
- Routines and rules have taken control
- Leaders are torn between many priorities

Scattered collaboration: low awareness, high focus. Private agendas determine work.

- People move in different directions and miss opportunities
- Teams miss out on synergies and only follow orders
- Leaders follow their own agendas

Random collaboration: low awareness, low focus. People cooperate where there is trust.

- People don't know what's important and who to go to for information
- Teams work in isolation without getting things done
- Leaders are uncertain and out of their depth, and tend to keep their heads down

Strategies for reaching the flow line of superior collaboration include mobilizing energy, building trust and facilitating collaboration. The solution involves the following:

- **Build awareness and focus attention on collaboration**: Use agile systems (with management by objectives that work, rules and routines, and collaboration tools) and marshal leaders to work *in* the system (see Chapter 1).
- **Remove interference**: Fix erroneous systems, remove faulty leadership and train leaders – the agile way.

Take the Collaboration Break on the next page to review what you can do about cooperation in your organization.

This section introduced the elements that determine your organization's growth capacity: collaboration, purpose and relationships. Stakeholders have expectations. You can use them to identify your organization's growth ambitions.

MY COLLABORATION BREAK

 What are your challenges? Use your results from the Agile Diagnostic (Tool #4).

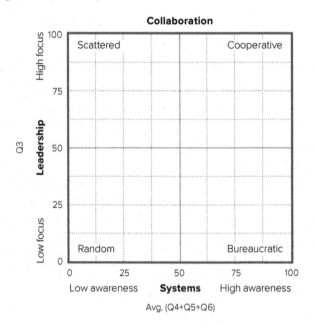

 How will you get to the flow line? Where is your potential, and what interference do you face?

 What are your gaps and what strategies will help you to close the gaps?

#5 OPERATIONS

The operations dimension captures the necessary capabilities to compete in the new environment and the outcomes that you can expect from managing your operation the agile, people-centric and dynamic way. This section compares your organization's dynamic capabilities with the outcomes that you can expect from agile and people-centricity.

It is increasingly recognized that companies need to be fast, agile and resilient. Speed represents the capacity to implement strategy quickly. Agility provides "the capacity to consistently change without having to change. It is the efficiency with which we can respond to non-stop change and resilience adds stability as the capacity to absorb, react to, and potentially reinvent the business model as a consequence of change. Speed, agility, and resilience describe the elements of an organization's dynamic capabilities. Such organizations enable people to perform the inner game and create the capabilities to cope with a volatile environment, the outer game" (Anzengruber, 2013).

The Performance Triangle (see Figure 13) suggests that speed, agility and resilience are the ultimate dynamic capabilities required to compete and collaborate in today's world. These capabilities will help you to address changes in the environment without the negative effects of traditional change programmes.

Speed and control: The 'individual environment' of the Performance Triangle defines how we engage with people. The inner game is the technique that helps people to translate knowledge into action. It transfers control to the learner. Learning is the solution for time-critical action in dynamic times. Trust and choice relate to speed and creative capabilities. Speed must be balanced with control.

Agility and stability: The 'operating environment' of the Performance Triangle defines how we coordinate work. Agility is all about sensing opportunities early, taking action and continuously implementing change through an integrated organization. It promotes self-organized work in teams with delegated decision-making for higher flexibility, effective adaptation to external change, improved problem-solving and superior innovation as its benefits. Agility requires a combination of dynamic managerial capabilities and managerial controls. Agility must be balanced with stability.

Resilience and renewal: The 'work environment' of the Performance Triangle defines how we establish goals as a bonding element of relationships. It has a stabilizing effect through social controls and the ability to absorb volatility and shocks. Resilience is about the 'robustness' of systems. Organizations reach higher levels of resilience through using purpose and relationships as cooperative strategies. They are able to reinvent themselves and find new business models that preserve their core. The way we set goals determines much about our relationships with stakeholders and the growth of our organization. Resilience must be balanced with renewal.

These capabilities are the sources of organizational outcomes: performance, innovation and growth (Figure 20).

FIGURE 20: THE OPERATIONS DIMENSION

Performance: The inner game is the technique that translates knowledge into action and transfers control to the learner. Awareness, choice and trust help people to focus on what counts. The result is flow (Csikszentmihalyi, 1990) – the state in which learning, performance and joy collide to deliver superior results.

Innovation: Innovation and agility are strongly correlated. We know that innovative organizations have agile capabilities, and agile capabilities lead to superior innovations. It's the classic chicken-and-egg problem. What matters is that agile capabilities lead to superior innovation. In an environment where people can unlock their creativity and create new knowledge, innovation is the outcome.

Growth: Purpose, relationships and collaboration have the capacity to absorb and renew. By using cooperative strategies, businesses can reinvent themselves with new business models while they preserve their core. The way we set goals and how we deal with stakeholders determine much of the internal growth capacity of a company.

The Operations Dimension Break will help you to explore your organizational capabilities and outcomes: speed and control, agility and stability, resilience and renewal, performance, innovation and growth.

MY OPERATIONS DIMENSION BREAK

 What are your challenges? Use your results from the Agile Diagnostic (Tool #4).

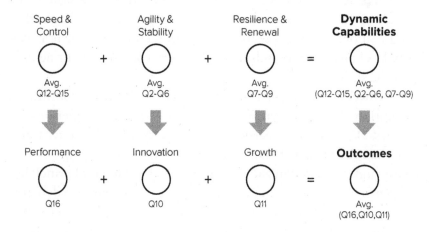

 Where is your potential, and what interference do you face?

What are the operational key issues that require your attention?

AGILE MATURITY

Your agile maturity level is a gauge that can be used to review the agility of your organization. It is calculated using the average of the Dynamic Capabilities and Outcome scores from the Agile Diagnostic (Tool #4) and produces a ranking on a scale of six levels, from pioneers at the top to contestants at the bottom. The scale is the result of 15 years of research with my organization's diagnostics and 250 organizations worldwide in all sectors. Your agile maturity level gives you an indication of where you are in your people-centric shift.

Pioneers are designed in such a way as to ensure continuous evolution. They use dynamic capabilities to deliver superior outcomes. Decentralized decision-making, teamwork and active influence are the trademarks of a new way to manage – the agile way – with guided self-organization as one of its fundamental principles.

Performers are designed in such a way as to encourage a dynamic environment. They have built capabilities that enable them to navigate in a VUCA (volatile, uncertain, complex and ambiguous) world and that balance people's needs and organizational objectives. Coordination across boundaries, self-control and connectivity help them to outdo their peers, even in a turbulent context, on performance, innovation and growth.

Enablers are designed in such a way as to engage well with people in a stable environment. These organizations motivate people based on self-responsibility, purpose and social control. They favour action orientation and knowledge work. However, their implementation of the people-centric approach is insufficient to cope with a dynamic setting. The fix is to implement radically decentralized decision-making.

Changers are designed in such a way as to implement disruptive change. Whenever their leaders believe that change is required, they alter their structures and reallocate resources. As the context changes, they keep restructuring. The fix is always more control, direct managerial influence and relentless customer focus.

Exploiters are designed in such a way as to exploit their assets. They optimize processes to deliver at the lowest possible level of asset utilization. Many are quite successful in doing so.

Consequently, their leaders are satisfied with the current situation. However, in dynamic markets, they don't have the capabilities to adapt quickly. They can fix their situation by tightening performance management and embarking on change.

Contestants have inherited a design based on operating in a stable environment. Often, their context and current capabilities don't match, and this reflects an infected culture, faulty leadership or erroneous systems. Typical but ineffective resolutions include fixing the culture, people and leaders. Contestants are stuck in bureaucracy.

Take your Agile Maturity Break on the next page to determine your position on the scale.

MY AGILE MATURITY BREAK

 What are your challenges? Use your results from the Agile Diagnostic (Tool #4).

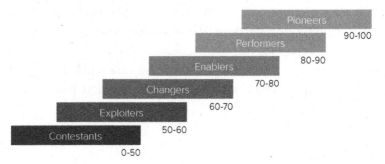

Pioneers 90-100
Performers 80-90
Enablers 70-80
Changers 60-70
Exploiters 50-60
Contestants 0-50

 Where is your potential, and what interference do you face?

What are the operational key issues that require your attention?

MENTORING

So far, you have considered agile according to five dimensions: people, the organization, management, work and operations. You have further evaluated the elements and reviewed your organization's agile maturity. Given your challenges, your strategy, your business model and your management model, you have likely found that your organization needs to work on its agile capabilities. And working on something starts with having the right design.

Agile is a capability that needs design. This section guides your 'work *on* the system' through mentoring, using the canvas to capture your design results.

Mentoring (Figure 21) applies the inner game to design. The self-mentoring process is central to *Agile by Choice*. It is the same approach that my organization's agile experts use when they work with their executive clients. As such, mentoring follows the same principles that establish the foundation of agile leadership, organization and management: awareness, insights and learning.

Mentoring has three stages and comes with a variety of tools (Figure 22) that offer nudges on your agile journey from your current to your future reality.

Awareness (Focus)	**Insights** (Choice)	**Learning** (Trust)
Sensing, agile diagnostics, observation points	Knowing, agile dimensions and models, shared language, intervention points	Transforming, agile expertise, leverage points

FIGURE 21: MENTORING STAGES

Awareness: Diagnostics are the sensing tools that help you to see the invisible: your potential and the interference that keeps you from delivering your expected outcomes. Observation points help you to identify the systemic relationships between the critical agile elements of your organization to distil your dominant assumptions, principles and patterns. Awareness turns opinions into meaning to create purpose.

Insights: The five dimensions – people, organization, work, operations and management – in line with the Performance Triangle (Michel, 2013) model create a shared language on agile. With the help of the Nudges and breaks throughout the book, you can identify the critical intervention points and articulate your ideal design with gaps and key issues. Your design choices will take you from symptoms to root causes with clarity on where to interfere.

Learning: Expertise will help you to transform your organization and develop agile at scale. Trust yourself to identify the initiatives that will offer the most leverage on how to switch from idea to action. Establish a roadmap for how you and your team can collaborate, using your management skills to create superior value.

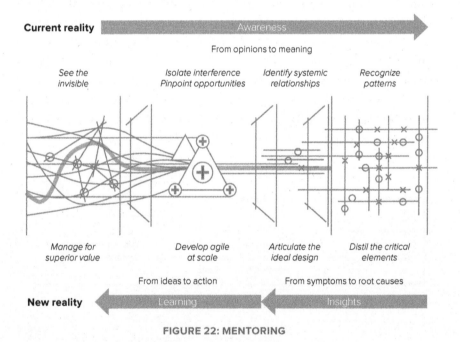

FIGURE 22: MENTORING

THE CANVAS

The canvas (Figure 23) documents the five dimensions in a template with questions that you can use to capture your design ideas and results. Five pairs of questions guide your design. Within each pair, the first question is about work *on* the system while the second question guides your work *in* the system. The switch from question one to question two prepares you to transition from your individual journey to a journey that you make with your team and the entire organization.

- **People**: How do I engage people? How do we know with clarity?
- **Organization**: How do I coordinate work? How do we move in one direction?
- **Work**: How do I mobilize the energy? How do we mobilize resources?
- **Operations**: How do I enable development? How do we maintain the focus?
- **Management**: How do I manage the organization? How do we lead the people-centric way?

The canvas is your notes for your agile journey. Use it as follows:

- **Assumptions, principles and potential** (green stickers) and **interference** (red stickers): the Agile Diagnostic (Tool #4) offers the relevant observation points
- **Gaps** (yellow stickers): the difference between your current situation and your desired situation indicates the gaps that require your attention
- **Key issues** (dark blue stickers): the themes that you have decided to work on indicate your focus areas
- **Initiatives** (grey stickers): these translate key issues into initiatives that help you to address the key issues
- **Roadmap** (bright blue stickers): this schedules and resources initiatives into a programme that will ensure that your organization makes the transition to agile

The canvas (Tool #6, Document Agile) is a template that can be used as a poster to work with a team in a workshop setting. The use of coloured stickers helps to separate the above steps.

Alongside the canvas, use Tool #6, Document Agile, to take a Canvas Break and capture your design ideas using the canvas template.

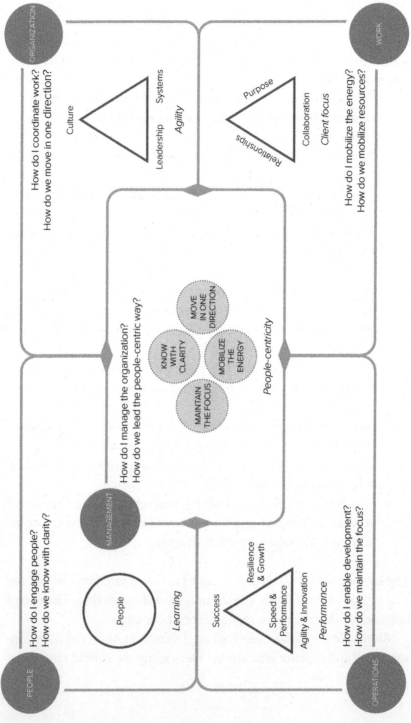

FIGURE 23: THE CANVAS

MY CANVAS BREAK

 What are assumptions, principles, the potential and interferences? Use your results from the Agile Diagnostic (Tool #4) and the canvas template, Tool #6, Document Agile.

 What are the key issues that address the gaps?

 What are initiatives and the roadmap to implement the key issues?

THE AGILE CHOICE

Having made the choice of agile, it is now time to switch from working *on* the system to working *in* the system. This is the transition from the design mode to the doing mode. Figure 24 summarizes the transition in five parts.

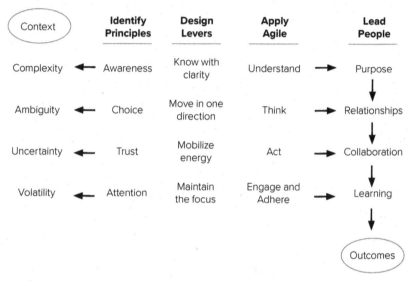

FIGURE 24: YOUR AGILE CHOICE

Understand context: In the context of increasing complexity, ambiguity, uncertainty and volatility, agile capabilities help your organization to quickly adapt to the new environment. They resolve the tensions between the challenges of the new context and the need for clarity, direction, energy and focus. This part is about raising awareness in your team that the context has changed, which encourages the search for agile capabilities.

Identify principles: People are well-equipped to resolve the tensions the new context poses. They can apply four principles derived from the inner game – awareness, choice, trust and attention – to address the challenges of the outer game. This part is about your choice of people-centric management in line with these principles. Applying the inner game is about mindset and has implications for the design of the four people-centric levers: self-organization, delegation, self-responsibility and focus of attention (see Section #3 in this chapter).

Design levers: The concepts of knowing with clarity, moving in one direction, mobilizing resources and maintaining the focus offer a choice between traditional and people-centric management. This part is about your decision to pursue people-centric management by choosing the four people-centric levers. It's a choice with implications for your leaders' skillset.

Apply agile: Following people-centric management calls for five managerial tasks: understand, think, act, engage and adhere. This part requires you to make a decision on your Leadership Scorecard and Toolbox[2] with rules, routines and tools that leaders in your organization use at scale to perform the four tasks. You will have to think about the most appropriate design of your systems, leadership and culture.

Lead people: With the right design of your toolbox, your leaders will establish purpose as the source of motivation, connect people to nurture relationships, facilitate collaboration as a means to coordinate work, and expedite learning as the means for performance, innovation and growth.

PRIORITIES

The five leadership dimensions can help you to establish leadership everywhere and to embed people-centric and agile capabilities at scale with the right priorities in mind (Figure 25). Leadership everywhere is the mandate, with people first (the inner game and learning), the organization second (the elements of the agile Performance Triangle), management third (four people-centric levers), work fourth (the focus on clients) and operations fifth (dynamic capabilities and outcomes).

The choice of agile establishes an environment with five priorities. Keep this in mind while you work *on* the system.

Modern employees are all executives: They make decisions. Leadership everywhere is the code for self-responsible people who know with clarity, self-organized teams that move in one direction, delegation that mobilizes energy, and broad direction that maintains the focus. As a leader, it must be your goal to engage people, delegate and establish leadership everywhere.

Your organization sets the context: Agile capabilities enable people-centric management. Systems, leadership and culture establish the necessary operating environment for people to apply their talent and perform. Hence, it is important to be clear about the potential and the interference in your organization.

People are the centre of your attention: People-centric principles demand an individual environment where people can unlock their talent and perform at their peak. It is people who deliver value to clients. They should be able to experience flow – the state where challenges and capabilities meet to create a positive experience. That is the ultimate goal of people-centric management. As a leader, it is your task to create that kind of work environment.

It is people who care about clients: People-centric principles enable you as a leader to demand self-responsibility, delegate work, enable self-organization and lead with broad directives. This means that the people in your organization can take charge and take care of clients. Client focus is all about your people making sure that valuable clients come back and want more.

Success is what attracts owners: Owners look for growth and return on their investment. Growth comes from clients who come back. Returns come from efficiency gains and innovations. Long-term value creation must be the goal of the business.

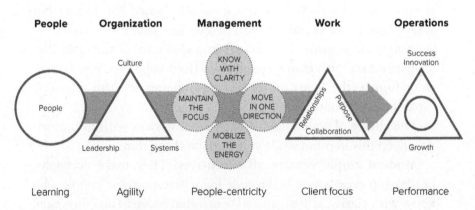

FIGURE 25: THE FIVE LEADERSHIP DIMENSIONS

THE AGILE JOURNEY OF
SEVEN EXECUTIVES

Having now thoroughly introduced agile, let us return to the agile journeys of the seven executives. They have all reached the stage of greater awareness for agile with clarity on what needs to happen:

The chief executive of the large insurance company's task was to gather all support staff around a shared agile agenda to promote entrepreneurship throughout the organization. The CEO's intent was to create awareness and a shared language around entrepreneurship. He asked 100 managers from the US, Europe and Asia to complete the online Agile Diagnostic[3] with a focus on the Performance Triangle model. Via a video-supported workshop occurring simultaneously in New York, Zürich and Singapore, he engaged all participants (including his support staff) in a conversation about the critical elements of agility (according to the Performance Triangle) and what it takes for each talent to become more entrepreneurial. Another expert staff briefing workshop with the support staff translated the outcomes of the leadership workshop into a roadmap that could be used to alter managerial systems and train all executives globally on the use of the agile approach based on self-responsibility and engagement. The insights from the diagnostic established a shared language and high awareness of the need for a successful shift to people-centricity.

The manager of the global pharmaceutical company's task was to initiate agile with the company's management team in order to re-establish innovation. Eight managers in the US, Europe and Asia were asked to conduct the online Agile Diagnostic with a focus on innovation. The results revealed considerable gaps in agile capabilities in all regions they managed that prevented any innovation from occurring. It became clear that the organization needed a different approach to management, with more agile routines that it was used to. Additionally, the initial diagnostic exercise revealed something that the company's manager did not expect: the managers' style was to let things go and trust the talent. Agile, on the other hand, demands another kind of discipline from the talent – but with an equal amount of rigour. Agile is not the easy way out. Through intensive coaching and positive experiences with agile procedures, the manager was able to grasp what agile was all about. Once he had that higher level of awareness, he involved all his managers in discussing the diagnostic results, distilled the critical issues, and created a roadmap that would turn his company's traditional approach into an agile approach to stimulate creativity and innovation.

The architect and chief of staff of a global think-tank faced the challenge of engaging the organization's executive team in a conversation about agile management. Given the context of a dominant founder and an executive team that resisted anything that did not come from the world's top three consulting companies or supporters of the think-tank, it was unrealistic to ask the team to conduct the online Agile Diagnostic. However, they agreed to attend a workshop to discuss agile. The architect therefore translated the digital diagnostic into an analogue version, with posters that included the same details. The workshop participants were then asked to spend 30 minutes of the meeting going through the posters and answering the diagnostic questions. After five minutes, the conversations had already become so intense and rich that there was no need to go through the entire process. The process established an awareness of agile and many valuable insights.

The translator and CEO office manager of a South African food producer had the task of translating between the agile aspirations of the CEO and the management reality of the company in a traditional quality-and-control environment. As mandated by the CEO, 20 managers from across the organization conducted the online Agile Diagnostic. As expected, the people-centric aspect of the diagnostic revealed a very traditional management context. The Leadership Scorecard and Toolbox favoured rigour over agility. During the team workshop it became clear to all of the participants that they needed a hybrid model in which they could apply traditional approaches to their operations but employ agile strategic thinking when they gathered to discuss the future of the company. The CEO office manager was challenged to redesign some of the strategy and performance management processes that guided the work of the executive team. She had to translate the hybrid context into a process that was able to handle both traditional and agile approaches.

The integrator and manager of the mid-sized city in the US had to get all managers involved in a process that would change the culture and make the city more agile and service friendly. He arranged for 1,250 employees, from gardeners to IT specialists and airport employees, to complete the online Agile Diagnostic. The results covered 12 departments, and the city manager then conducted a workshop with 35 key leaders as a train-the-trainer event. The participants learned how to interpret the data from the diagnostic and conduct a conversation around agility, and were able to distil the critical elements that would make them more agile and citizen friendly. These leaders then used their own department's results and conducted the same workshops with their supervisors and employees. They gained experience as they were doing agile. In this way, the city manager integrated the learning into the day-to-day work of all city employees.

The chair of the Middle Eastern sugar company needed to create a scalable model that would support the onboarding of new managers to capture ongoing growth. As might be expected, agile was not the primary concern of the founder of one of the world's largest sugar plants. But without talking much about agile, agile structures, agile role descriptions, and basic agile metrics, strategy, performance and risk processes guided the first three years of the company's existence. After years three and five, the company's management team completed the online Agile Diagnostic to ensure that the organization remained on track with its development. The chair used team workshops to review the diagnostic's results and, at the same time, train new members on how to manage their operations without hampering growth.

The executive coach with global clients made the choice of agile. We know that it takes the transformed to initiate transformations. Agile diagnostics and visual design thinking[4] helped her to raise awareness of agile among her clients by initiating the process with the leader. She used many of the thought processes in this book to work with her clients on being first in coaching to make the change to agile.

Awareness and insights are the keys to initiating the people-centric shift. The stories of the seven executives will be continued in Chapter 6.

In this chapter, we have explored the five dimensions of agile with a focus on the elements in your organization that require your attention. If it all went well, you must now have made your choice of agile. In the next chapter, we will return to you as an individual in your executive role and further explore the inner game.

FIVE LEADERSHIP DIMENSIONS

People-centricity, agile and dynamism are the essential individual, managerial and organizational capabilities required to succeed in today's world. Five dimensions – people, organization, management, work and operations – offer the critical elements that help you establish leadership everywhere.

KEY CHAPTER IDEAS

- People with knowledge are executives who play the inner game
- The Performance Triangle's elements identify agile in organizations
- Four levers establish people-centric management
- The client focus comes from balancing stakeholder interests
- Dynamic capabilities offer the outcomes for sustainable value creation
- People-centric, agile and dynamic capabilities need design

ACTION AGENDA

- Use the results of the Agile Diagnostic (Tool #4) to identify your leadership dimensions and elements

FURTHER READING

On the people dimension: Gallwey, W. T. (2000). *The Inner Game of Work*. New York: Random House.

On the organization dimension: Michel, L. (2013). *The Performance Triangle: Diagnostic Mentoring to Manage Organizations and People for Superior Performance in Turbulent Times.* London: LID Publishing.

On the work dimension: Neely, A., Adams, C. and Kennerly, M. (2002). *The Performance Prism: The Scorecard for Measuring and Managing Business Success.* London: Financial Times/Prentice Hall.

On the management dimension: Michel, L. (2020). *People-centric Management: How Leaders Use Four Levers to Bring Out the Greatness of Others.* London: LID Publishing.

On design: Michel, L. (2017). *Management Design: Managing People and Organizations in Turbulent times* (2nd ed.). London: LID Publishing.

CHAPTER 3

The Inner Game

In art, science, sports and work, playing the inner game enables people to better use their resources – for example, unlock their ability to learn quickly, make better decisions and perform at their peak. This chapter offers a nudge for you to explore how the principles of the inner game can be used as techniques to help you make the shift to people-centricity and coach your team to establish agile throughout your organization.

NUDGE #3: ENGAGE YOUR INNER GAME
Use the principles of awareness, choice and trust to reach
flow with your thinking and choice of agile.

The inner game[5] provides techniques to help people cope with higher challenges: doubts, stress, fear, biased focus, limiting concepts and assumptions can distort our thoughts, decisions, behaviours and actions. This keeps us from always operating at our full potential. The art of relaxing our distorting thoughts is called the inner game. Here is a brief introduction.

Experience vs. instruction: The inner game is an organic and natural learning process based on experience. Attention and focus help us to learn by doing things, applying our own experience. This is in sharp contrast to learning by instruction. Instruction is external control. Most instructions compromise the natural abilities of the learner.

Self 1 and Self 2 (Figure 26): The voice of giving commands and making judgements is what we call 'Self 1.' 'Self 2' is yourself. Self 1 is the know-it-all who does not trust Self 2. Self 2 is the one who actually performs, although it is challenged by the mistrust implied by the judgement of Self 1. The self-doubt and over-control interfere with the natural learning process. Self 2 is the human being itself, with all its inherent potential and the innate ability to learn.

The material and quantum worlds: In our three-dimensional everyday environment, objects, people, space and time dominate as matter. Our focus on the material world consumes energy, with the result that this energy is not available for new things. Routine and habits prevail. Influencing the world through matter takes time. Space and time are different. You are here, the future is there. Focusing on the past and future consumes our energy. In the quantum world, infinite energy is available. Space collapses in infinite time: the defining moment. It's the home of the energy self. When we redirect attention from the outside, material world, the self activates. This allows us to move from Self 1 to Self 2 and beyond. We can access our full potential and possibilities.

Dominant patterns: Our stock of behavioural patterns, which we have accumulated over the years, guides everything we do. This is comfortable, as much of what we do consumes little energy and needs no mental effort. It consists of habits. Our stock of habits protects us from dangers and unpleasant experiences. This mechanism is automatic and always present.

The cycle of self-interference: Perception, response and results are part of every action we take. We have an image of what needs to be done. Then we respond by performing. This produces the result, which is the action. Between perception (the image) and the action (the response) there is room for interpretation. Meaning is attached to every action and often to the performer themselves. These meanings impact the actor's performance. Self 1 introduces distortion into every part of the action: distorted perception, distorted response, distorted results, distorted self-image. There must be a better way of dealing with the performer's distortions.

Self 1	Self 2
Interference that limits my potential	Everything that enables me to use my full potential
Doubts, stress, fear, bias, limiting concepts and assumptions	Resources, skills, attitude

FIGURE 26: SELF 1 AND SELF 2

INNER AND OUTER INTERACTIONS

The context in which we perform, learn and work has a huge impact on how effective and satisfying our work is. The external context certainly matters. But the inner game suggests that the space between our own ears matters even more. All our thoughts, feeling, values, assumptions, definitions, attitudes, desires and emotions matter when it comes to performing demanding tasks or thoughts. When goals, obstacles and critical variables for success are clear, then performance happens in a fulfilling way. But when internal conflicts dominate, when thoughts and feelings pull in different directions, it's not easy stay on track. Priorities become blurred, commitments are compromised, and doubts, fears and self-limitations rule. Figure 27 suggests three simultaneous interactions to consider.

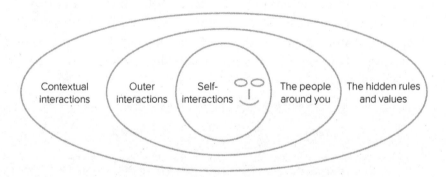

FIGURE 27: THREE PERSONAL INTERACTIONS

Self-interactions do not exist in isolation. They are influenced by the outer interactions we have with the people around you. For example, the quality of your relationships with your boss, your team at work or your sports team impacts how you perform. An insecure boss may overuse control, which impacts the self-confidence of individuals and teams. This then limits both individual and team interactions and performance.

Another interaction also impacts how we work and perform: the conversations that silently happen in the back of your mind. It consists of the hidden rules, values and assumptions that arise from the culture of our context. Corporate culture, for example, shapes the way we think, behave and act in a positive or negative way. While culture often is the source of all trouble, it is hard to change.

The self-interactions: Many things influence our thinking and thereby get in the way of performance. As humans, we have ample skills, potential and room to think. But Self 1 interference, the invented self, is the voice that is fed by sources outside us and sows doubts that undermines us. Self-doubts lead to fear, judgements, over-control and internal conflicts that disrupt the inner environment in which we perform. This voice sounds like it is coming from a parent, a teacher, a boss or a friend who knows how to conform to the norms and rules within the context that determines the game we play. Self 1 is a voice that wants me, Self 2, to accept that it dictates what I think and do independent of my own experience and understanding. Listening to Self 2 – the innate, natural self – is an essential challenge of the inner game. A harmonious relationship with Self 2 requires an internal conversation based on clarity, trust and choice.

The outer interactions: The purpose of the inner game is to quiet Self 1 such that it does not interfere with Self 2. Another person can hinder or help the process, either by augmenting Self 1's disruption or facilitating Self 2's natural functioning. The inner game works by introducing a different conversation than the one with Self 1. Rather than judgement, there is objective observation: things are what they are. For Self 2, the place of doubt or control is taken by trust. Manipulation is replaced by choice. The goal is to shift from a disruptive, confused and self-critical state of mind to one that is focused.

The contextual interactions: Fear, control and power are viruses (see Tool #1) that can pervade a corporate culture. These invisible conversations have great influence on performance as they may lead to stress and conflicts, often with unintended consequences.

Recognizing the relationships between the three interactions – the self-interactions, the outer interactions and the contextual interactions – enables you to change these interactions. To accomplish productive, unhindered self-interactions, you must become aware of yourself, your team and (most challengingly) the context within which you operate.

Awareness, choice and trust help you to deal with interference – the self-made and the external:

- **Non-judgemental awareness is incredibly powerful**, but too often many of our managerial sensors are on mute.
- **The choice of how to perform an action should reside with the performer**, but organizations need to establish boundaries on choice, otherwise people may exceed their allotted space to manoeuvre.
- **Trust in Self 2 is the fastest management concept**, but most organizations are built on mistrust.
- **Focus of attention**: this is the key to learning and performance, but we continue to aim at everything that moves.

PLAYING THE INNER GAME

TRUSTING SELF 2

When you are in the flow and rhythm of Self 2, you are inherently satisfied. It gives you the feeling that everything is working and things are coming together. When you experience that state, you naturally try to keep it – or, if you lose it, you try to make it return. But this usually does not work instantly.

When we lose focus, there is conflict between Self 1 and Self 2. What can we do? If we use Self 1 strategies to control Self 2, we will strengthen the task master that is causing the conflict. If we try to resist Self 1, the interference gets stronger. If we focus on Self 2, we delay its return.

The way to succeed is to trust in Self 2. Acknowledging Self 2 means that you give it any attention you want to. As attention is a scare resource, giving more attention to Self 2 reduces the attention given to Self 1. Simultaneously, this opens up the resources that you have available from Self 2.

IGNORING SELF 1

Self 1 is creative and subtle in the strategies and techniques it uses to interfere. And it's easy to use Self 1 to distract anyone else's Self 2. The examples of successes are endless. Self 1's whispers are just around the corner. Some mean them well; others use them to their own advantage. Whether it is to undermine confidence or build up an ego, all they have to do is to command a certain amount of attention from their victims. The only way to make the inner game beneficial for all parties is to make the decision to tune out Self 1. Focus is the best defence and best offence against interference from Self 1.

THE WORK ENVIRONMENT

The following simple formula defines the inner game:

Performance = Potential – Interference

Self 2 represents the great potential in yourself, your team and your organization. Only interference through Self 1 can limit people's performance. Hence, we need to pay attention to the process of limiting the negative effects of Self 1: self-doubt, erroneous assumptions and fear of failure.

Figure 28 bridges people, organization and context at work to show the challenges of the outer game that people and organizations accept. "The greater the external challenges accepted by a company, team or individual, the more important it is that there is minimum interference occurring from within" (Gallwey, 2000). In this light, the job of the leader is to create a work environment that limits the negative effects of Self 1 so that Self 2 can accept higher challenges. But "resistance to change within the corporation is rooted in the prevailing command and control corporate culture" (Gallwey, 2000).

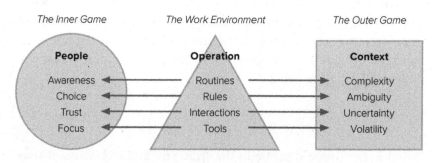

FIGURE 28: THE WORK ENVIRONMENT

In contrast, work environments where people can focus on Self 2 are designed differently:

- **Routines** are the means for people to address complexity. To cope with growing complexity, routines need to create awareness rather than control.
- **Rules** help people to deal with ambiguity. In times of increasing ambiguity, rules must enable choice.

- **Interactions** between leaders and employees must reduce uncertainty. To cope with rising levels of uncertainty, leader needs to trust rather than command.
- **Tools** must deal with volatility. To address greater volatility, tools must focus attention rather than aim at goals.

Applying the inner game in practice will teach you that losing focus is easy as you can be distracted. At work, distractions are everywhere. Maintaining focus is not a matter of losing it but a matter of shortening how long it takes you to regain focus. The best strategy is to practise getting your focus back quickly.

It is now time to take the Inner Game Break on the next page.

MY CANVAS BREAK

 What are your challenges? Use your results from the Agile Diagnostic (Tool #4).

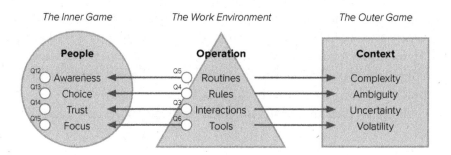

The Inner Game — *The Work Environment* — *The Outer Game*

People	Operation	Context
Awareness	Routines	Complexity
Choice	Rules	Ambiguity
Trust	Interactions	Uncertainty
Focus	Tools	Volatility

 Where is your potential, and what interference do you face?

⊕ What are the key issues that require your attention?

FLOW

Flow (Csikszentmihalyi, 1990) is a concept that is related to the inner game. It is a personal zone where challenges, skills and performance collide to offer a state in which a person performing an activity is fully immersed, has energized focus, and feels full involvement in and enjoyment of the activity. It is Self 2 in action without the interference of Self 1. Figure 29 shows this defining moment or flow zone.

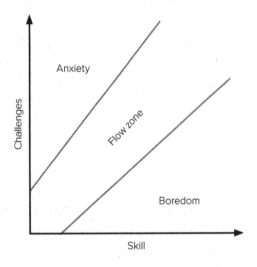

FIGURE 29: FLOW

"Flow also happens when a person's skills are fully involved in overcoming a challenge that is just about manageable, so it acts as a magnet for learning new skills and increasing challenges," Csikszentmihalyi (1990) explains. He continues, "If challenges are too low, one gets back to flow by increasing them. If challenges are too great, one can return to the flow state by learning new skills... The best moments in our lives are not the passive, receptive, relaxing times...

The best moments usually occur if a person's body or mind is stretched to its limits in a voluntary effort to accomplish something difficult and worthwhile."

Flow is a defining moment. It's when our mind switches from the material world (matter) to the quantum world (energy). In the here and now, the past and future collapse into the present. It's where time is infinite and eternal, and space has unlimited dimensions. To reach flow, we need to leave the physical world and body to become a self with infinite possibilities. In this way, we access our true potential. Reaching the state of flow in the here and now requires practice. Awareness and focus of attention are the techniques used to get there.

Flow occurs when we switch from the beta state (thinking mind) to the relaxed and creative alpha state. Most of the day, our brains are governed by the frequency of beta waves. We are awake and our senses are aware. At times, we switch to the alpha state, in which we are quiet, relaxed, creative and intuitive without thinking and analysing. We are dreaming. In the beta state we focus on the environment, whereas in the alpha state the focus is on us, the inner self.

Too much challenge, not enough safety: Anxiety is everywhere in the workplace as everyone has too much to do and not enough time to accomplish it. It is the classic situation of losing focus. Everyone and everything demands our attention. One way to ease this situation is to reduce the amount of unnecessary interference from Self 1 concerning things like perfection, over-control and avoidance of risk. Limiting that interference frees up attention capacity for Self 2. Staying focused is the only way to work effectively and efficiently.

Too little challenge, too much safety: When a job demands too little of us or a task is perceived as routine or unimportant, our focus can be taken over by a sense of boredom. We perceive that we are undervalued and that our capabilities are unused, and this shuts down the receptors of the nervous system, resulting in a condition of non-alertness. This leads to disengagement, with the conclusion that work is boring. Self 2 goes to sleep. The solution is to either bring challenges into work or find more meaningful work to do. Self 2 focus occurs when these inner conflicts are resolved or when all agendas are aligned.

STRESS

Stress interferes with performance and creativity. In situations where stress dominates, the 'prefrontal' (reflective) part of our brain turns off and the rear 'sensory cortex' (reactive) is activated. This means that in strongly stressful situations, reactivity dominates over reflectiveness. However, with only a little stress, the reflective mode dominates.

Stress switches our mind and body into survival mode. The primitive (sympathetic) nervous system is activated. Blood flow prioritises the reactive (rear) part of the brain over the reflective (front), with the result that we become primed to use routine and habit in order to react quickly. All our sensing mechanisms – seeing, hearing, feeling, smelling and sensing – are on alert. Our energy consumption is very high, with almost no capacity for creativity or new things.

In stressful situations, Self 1 interferes with Self 2. Boredom is too little stress, which reduces performance, and anxiety is too much stress, with the same effect. Figure 30 compares male and female stress. Men and women start from different stress levels and have different needs when it comes to optimal performance.

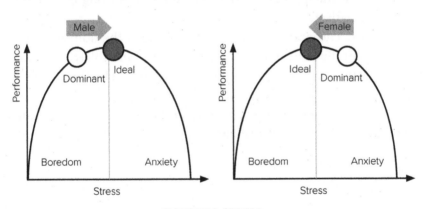

FIGURE 30: STRESS

In simplified terms, men's dominant stress level is slightly on the boredom side. For optimal performance they need a little push to increase their stress and performance. Women's dominant stress level indicates slight hyperactivity. For them, the ideal level of stress for optimal focus and performance comes from experiencing less pressure. Knowing this difference has huge implications for leadership and the design of the ideal work environment for the inner game. Losing focus moves a person's stress level towards the dominant position, and regaining lost focus moves it in the opposite direction. To regain focus, women need trust and men need motivation.

GETTING BACK INTO FOCUS

We must all balance a plethora of conflicting goals in both knowledge and physical work. They originate from lack of clarity and priorities about work. The result is confusion, in which focus is impossible. Distraction comes from unresolved conflict between priorities, in which other agendas than Self 2's agenda take over. Regaining lost focus can only come from higher awareness and concentration to quiet Self 1 and trust Self 2.

SETTING THE RIGHT PRIORITIES

Learning, enjoyment and performance are three interrelated components of goals (Figure 31). When the learning side of the triangle increases, it certainly impacts enjoyment and performance. Likewise, if enjoyment is decreased, this impacts learning and performance negatively.

In most corporate cultures, performance is the dominant goal component. But it is obvious to most people, that solely emphasizing performance does not lead to better results. The three sides of the triangle work together and part of our goal system. When one is ignored, the others suffer. When performance stalls, organizations push even harder on performance.

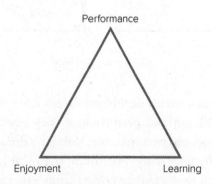

FIGURE 31: PRIORITIES

In the knowledge era, learning is a significant component of work. When people strongly like their jobs, it increases their ability to learn. Just getting the job done without increasing knowledge is not an option for people whose jobs relate to knowledge. Both performance and learning contribute to the overall results of the organization.

The enjoyment component is the least acknowledged of the three, as there is a widespread perception that work is not supposed to be enjoyable. But the belief that people should enjoy their work – for example, that they should find purpose in it – is slowly gaining more acceptance. Enjoyment is likely the dominant component in an era when talent is scarce.

LEARNING FROM EXPERIENCE

The inner game is all about learning from experience. You don't need any extra time to learn. It is done while you are performing your job. With frequent reflections on your learning experience, you can expedite the process. The choice of agile is a learning experience, which is another reason why I emphasize the importance of learning in this book.

FINDING YOUR FLOW ZONE

People who unlock their potential by balancing skills and challenges have passed the flow line and are performing in the zone. They are in a state where all three goals (performance, enjoyment and learning) combine to create undivided focus and attention. It is a state where knowledge, skills and emotions blend into the flow experience.

Passing the flow line involves a deliberate choice to achieve something special. It is a significant experience in which the moment releases a deep sense of achievement. It reinforces clarity and trust in our own capabilities, and it aligns feelings and thoughts about our goals.

Use Figure 32 to identify where you are on your way to flow.

Not yet reached the flow zone	In the flow zone
• You are reviewing options	• Your intent defines your priorities
• You reconsider your decisions	• You constantly search for new information that reinforces your intent
• It's hard to be motivated	• You mobilize all activities towards your purpose
• You cannot concentrate on important things	• You focus your attention – nothing can distract you from your intent
• It's hard to mobilize your energy	• You have no doubts about your intentions
• You have no image of your desired outcome	• You are clear about how to get to your destination
• You find interference everywhere	• Obstacles are a means to reinforce your efforts

FIGURE 32: FLOW – WHERE ARE YOU?

Figure 33 lists the things you can do to reach the flow zone:

Sharpen your ambition:
- Find a realistic goal
- The goal must move your emotions
- Keep it vague – no precision
- Clarify the goal as you go

Commit to performing:
- Commit your energy, time and attention
- When you reach the flow zone, take charge of state of mind and put your intent into action
- Resolve conflicts and contradictions concerning the direction of your intent
- Make sure both head and heart are with you

Safeguard the flow experience:
- Play the inner game to remain focused – don't get distracted, and build trust
- Reinforce positive energies

FIGURE 33: STEPS TO REACH THE FLOW ZONE

Keep limitations and potential sources of interference in mind. More often than not, your boundaries will be set by your client or boss. Figure 34 shows what you can do about this:

Unrealistic goals	Unacceptable conditions	Unused options
Establish your agenda	Frame your limits	Know your options
Reduce your aspirations, prioritize and organize	Accept contradictions	Expand your options
Structure your time	Break rules and habits	Learn
Manage expectations	Accept ambiguities and conflicts	Appreciate the degrees of freedom

FIGURE 34: SOURCES OF INTERFERENCE

It's now time for your Flow Break on the next page.

MY FLOW BREAK

 What are your goals? What are your priorities?

1. Score the importance of each goal (performance, enjoyment and learning) between 0 (Little importance) and 10 (High importance).
2. Plot your score into the triangle and connect your score into your triangle.

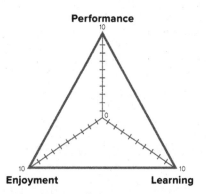

 Where is your flow zone?

 What can you do to experience flow more often? Use Tool #7, Get into the Flow.

All of our thoughts, decisions, actions and behaviours (Self 2) are distorted by self-made interference (Self 1) that pulls us in different directions, blurs our view, compromises our demands, or spreads fear and stress. At the same time, we need to cope with external sources of interference such as hurdles, blockages, pressures, an ineffective culture, others' expectations or the challenges of a difficult market environment. They all lead to higher volatility, uncertainty, complexity and ambiguity. As a result, these challenges prevent us from using our full potential.

Traditional management and organization are designed to promote efficiency. They are immune to our needs around natural thinking, deciding, performing and behaving. The only solution is to establish a work environment where people can unfold their knowledge and talents for the benefit of clients. The task is to close the gap between what people need to do (how they perform) and the benefits of agile design.

The principles of the inner game represent the people-centric foundations of how humans best manage and use their talents. As such, use the inner game to play your outer game, and coach your team to make agile their own choice. Flow is the result, and it:

- Balances challenges and skills
- Merges mind and body
- Clarifies goals through concentration and focus
- Provides clear and immediate feedback
- Concentrates on the now
- Provides superior control: a sense of power and trust
- Removes lock-in and releases inspiration
- Causes time to feel fluid
- Offers experiences where time and space dissolve

This section offered an introduction to the inner game and flow. The techniques in this section will help you to personally make the shift to people-centricity and coach your team to establish agile. In the following short sections, we will further review the elements of the inner game, recognizing their importance for the design of a work environment. We will start with awareness.

THE INNER GAME

In art, science, sports and work, playing the inner game enables people to better use their resources – for example, unlock their ability to learn quickly, make better decisions and perform at their peak.

KEY SECTION IDEAS

- The inner game follows the principles of awareness, trust and choice
- Flow is the state of peak performance where mind and body merge
- An agile work environment helps people to play the inner game

ACTION AGENDA

- Identify the elements of the inner game, flow and the work environment that can help you to shift to people-centricity (use Tool #7, Get into the Flow)

FURTHER READING

On the inner game: Gallwey, W. T. (2000). *The Inner Game of Work*. New York: Random House.

On flow: Csikszentmihalyi, M. (1990). *The Psychology of the Optimal Experience*. New York: Harper & Row.

AWARENESS

Awareness is part of the inner game: it is the insights we get from focused attention. Whatever the light of focus shines on becomes knowable and potentially understandable. Nudge #4 turns on the light and clears the fog obscuring our awareness. It offers sense-making as a tool to reach higher clarity. It demonstrates further why awareness is the means to cope with complexity and offers awareness as the first step of mentoring (see Part #5 of Chapter 2).

NUDGE #4: TURN ON YOUR LIGHTS
Use awareness to reach clarity on your thinking and choice of agile.

Complexity makes the search for valuable opportunities more difficult. Agility puts clients first. Step 1 of our management cycle, 'know with clarity' (see Section #3 of Chapter 2), ensures at scale throughout the organization that, despite high complexity, people can identify opportunities that will benefit clients through value creation. This benefits all other stakeholders.

How do we know with clarity? Awareness enables people to understand and engage with a deep sense of purpose. It is the key to managing in a complex environment – to knowing with clarity.

Awareness is about sensing by translating observed data into information without making a judgement about it. It is about having a clear understanding of the present. Non-judgemental awareness is the best way to sense what is going on. However, the more signals people receive, the more immune they become to the messages these signals contain.

THE POWER OF
NON-JUDGEMENTAL AWARENESS

When our Self 1 mind takes control of our thinking and determines our behaviours, we don't use our full potential. Interference takes over – either self-induced or as a defence mechanism against outside pressures. The golfer observes the green ahead of them by imagining the ball's flight; they respond to the situation by selecting the right golf club and act to produce the desired result by hitting the ball. It is a cycle of perception, response and results. We have the tendency to get in our own way – we start the cycle of distorted perception, distorted response and distorted results, which results in a distorted self-image. This negative spiral can be replaced by what can be called 'non-judgemental awareness.'

Once we realize that we are standing in our own way, we become aware that noticing 'what is' rather than 'what should be' is the key to removing interference. As a golfer, by simply observing the green ahead of you, you remove the threat that distorts your perception. By simply observing a specific thing during your swing, rather than telling your body what to do, you use your natural potential – remember, the swing always works on the driving range! By simply noticing the position of your ball, you acknowledge the result of your performance by accepting it. This is a cycle without any judgement and distortion of your self-image. It is a way to stop the cycle of self-interference.

The observation of a neutral but critical variable helps you to perform and improve an activity without any instruction. Watching your left foot during your golf swing helps you to keep the right balance without any distorting instruction. It is like magic; by using a critical performance variable at work, people steadily improve their performance. Learning takes place and performance improves. As a mentor, your only responsibilities are to maintain non-judgemental observation, provide opportunities to learn and ensure that people maintain their focus.

Awareness is about learning by translating data (through observation) into information without making a judgement about it. Awareness combines skills, knowledge and experience. Non-judgemental self-awareness is learning. Awareness is about knowing the present with clarity. Outside awareness is instruction. As a leader, you have an important policy choice to make between learning and instruction. Making this choice requires an understanding of how to provide direction and learn. It is a choice between being a coach who supports others' learning or a manager who tells people what to do.

SENSE-MAKING

Sense-making (Weick, 1995) is a tool that organizations can use at scale to reach higher levels of awareness. Good perception sharpens awareness of current reality. Awareness establishes a realistic view of the energy state of the organization. Shared awareness is a precondition for the credibility of the leadership team.

Sense-making is the means to understand emerging conditions and be part of an agile organization. Sense-making turns data into information to create a better understanding of the context in which decisions are made. It is an interaction tool that helps people to find responses to a question that arises in almost every decision-making situation: what does that (data, information) mean?

Sense-making focuses on the now, measurement and perception. The conversation includes understanding, questioning, insights and non-judgemental observation. It requires an attitude of learning, a sense of reality, development and focus. Access to relevant information and good feedback processes set the stage for effective sense-making. More information does not always help in an uncertain situation. In complex situations we need the right way to look at the information we have. Feedback is effective when it is immediate, consistent, self-directed, honest and controlled, and when it focuses on behaviours or performance and not the person.

How does sense-making work? According to Gary Klein (2009), "We make sense of data elements by fitting them into frames such as stories, but the reverse also happens – our frames determine what we use as data." Sense-making raises awareness of important things. It is more than just connecting the dots. It determines what counts next to the dots. To handle high complexity, we can rely on our cognitive ability to connect the dots and make meaning beyond the dots themselves.

THE ROLE OF OBSERVATION POINTS

Critical performance variables determine the focus points where our attention energy concentrates. Humans can naturally remember up to seven things, which limits the number of useful metrics. Knowing this enables organizations to respond practically. They can invest in selecting the right metrics rather than distracting people with long lists of what's important. Selecting and using performance metrics is a key ingredient in providing feedback in an agile organization. Done well, metrics guide organizations to observe the right things. Failing to meet critical performance metrics diverts attention, which means the organization loses focus, so it is crucial to only choose those metrics that are helpful to the organization's desired results.

STEPS TO REACH HIGHER AWARENESS

Feedback and information, in particular from critical performance variables, raise awareness of what is important. Non-judgemental observation helps us to translate data into meaningful information. Be relaxed. Simply focus on your observation points and learning will take place. This simultaneously eliminates all interference that keeps you from using your full potential. The defining moment will let you know your purpose with clarity.

Here are five steps to help you raise your awareness:

1. **Be aware**: The better your ability to focus your attention, the quicker and easier it is to reach clarity. Reaching clarity is easier than maintaining it.
2. **Focus attention**: The clearer your definition of your goal, the easier it will be to reach. Clarity on your goal opens up further options. Having more options increases the probability of a valuable solution.
3. **It's your choice**: How you deal with your emotions may lead to clarity in challenging situations.

4. **Trust your intuition**: To quickly reach clarity on challenging decisions, it helps to view different perspectives and use to your intuition.
5. **Visualize your intent**: Visualizing the future mobilizes the energy to get there. This kind of visualization is a capability that most leaders need to develop.

Use Tool #8, Create Awareness, to reach higher awareness.

COMPLEXITY

Complexity increases with size as we add employees, locations, products, segments, functions and stakeholders to our organization. The challenge in traditional organizations is that when we lose sight of what truly matters, we ask for more detail and more precision. We install complex processes and still look in the wrong direction. Agile processes enable us to cope with the complexity of organizations.

Awareness is the light that helps us to reach clarity and better cope with complexity. The agile solution is to consider the options for how managers can help people to find purpose. The use of information tools facilitates shared understanding at scale throughout an organization.

The awareness shift: To cope with growing complexity, routines need to create awareness rather than control. Complexity is like water; it cannot be compacted. Better awareness is the only way to deal with increased complexity. Traditional ways of addressing complexity include deconstructing it, setting goals and delegating decision-making. Increased complexity is a frequent cause of ineffective, bureaucratic routines and managerial processes. The fix is an appropriate design of routines that create awareness.

As an executive, create awareness: The inner game is about feedback and information, in particular from critical performance variables, which raise awareness of what is important. Non-judgemental observation helps you to translate data into meaningful information. Be relaxed. Simply focus on your observation points and learning will take place. This simultaneously eliminates all interference that keeps you from using your full potential. The defining moment will let you know your purpose with clarity.

Awareness in mentoring: Creating awareness and reaching clarity is the first phase of mentoring (see Part #5 of Chapter 2). With these inputs, refine clarity with your following Awareness Break.

MY AWARENESS BREAK

 What are your challenges in raising awareness? Use Tool #8, Create Awareness.

 What are the focus points that will help you to raise awareness?

How can you enable your organization to reach a high level of awareness, find purpose and know with clarity?

This section offered Nudge #4 and gave a brief introduction to awareness and to the tools that can help people to clear the fog and separate signals from the noise. Awareness is the key principle for addressing complexity in organizations. Your next nudge is about choice.

AWARENESS

Awareness comes from principles and tools that help us to tune our sensors and turn on the light to see what matters and address the complexity in our organization.

KEY SECTION IDEAS

- Non-judgemental awareness creates the feedback that enables learning
- Sense-making is the tool that enables greater awareness at scale in organizations
- Critical performance variables establish observation points
- Complexity is addressed via processes that enable higher levels of awareness
- The shift to people-centricity is initiated through higher awareness

ACTION AGENDA

- Take the steps required to personally reach higher levels of awareness by using Tool #8, Create Awareness
- Use awareness techniques to bring agile into your organization

FURTHER READING

On sense-making: Weick, K. (1995). *Sensemaking in organizations*. London: Sage.

On critical performance variables: Neely, A., Adams, C. and Kennerly, M. (2002). *The Performance Prism: The Scorecard for Measuring and Managing Business Success*. London: Financial Times/Prentice Hall.

CHOICE

Choice is another element of the inner game: it consists of deliberate decisions that follow our desires. It means pursuing what we like and saying no to the things that are not relevant to us. Nudge #5 makes the case that choice is the prerequisite for self-responsibility – the principle that brings all the joy of being human. This section offers tools to help you clarify your choice. It demonstrates that choice is needed to operate in an ambiguous environment.

NUDGE #5: IT'S YOUR CHOICE
Rely on Self 2 to make your choice of agile.

When we lose focus, there is confusion between Self 1 and Self 2. Self 1's strategies to control Self 2 only serve to give more voice to Self 1, which is the one that got us into trouble in the first place. The only strategy that works is to rely on Self 2, as this delays the return of Self 1. The choice of Self 2 gives access to attention and our own resources. This conscious choice diminishes Self 1's interference.

In an ambiguous market environment, making a decision on a valuable business opportunity is a challenge. Agile aims to guide decision-making without limiting choice. Step 2 of our management cycle, 'move in one direction' (see Section #3 of Chapter 2), offers that guidance at scale throughout the organization such that people make good choices that benefit clients and other stakeholder despite ambiguity.

How do we move in one direction? Choice is the prerequisite for assuming self-responsibility. But direction and choice do not naturally match. Self-responsibility is the choice to take charge and move in the desired direction.

WITHOUT CHOICE
THERE IS NO FREE WILL

Choice does not work unless there is a desired outcome. Any reaction to knowing a situation with clarity requires choice – the freedom to decide and the room to move. The first question is: who determines the outcome? It is one of the principles of the inner game that individuals make that choice and not the leader. They want to be responsible for their choice. Accountability implies taking charge of your own life. Giving the choice to the decision-maker makes the reasons behind the decision an important part of the learning process. Individuals feel in control and resistance is non-existent. They accept responsibility for the outcome.

Choice is about moving in the desired direction. Without choice, there is no free will. Making a choice requires options and an awareness of the pros and cons as well as the consequences of the choice. Purpose without a choice is meaningless.

People want to have choice. Whether people have opportunities to contribute is strongly linked to the amount of room they have to move and act. But the room to move requires space. Every space is defined by its boundaries. Without boundaries, there is no space. A lack of room to move is the same thing as a lack of opportunities to perform. Creating room to move means eliminating blockages such as rules, procedures and targets.

Choice means self-determination. It requires space with clear boundaries. Not providing choice means outside determination with rules and prescriptions. That is telling people what they should do and how they should do it.

Choice is about decision-making. In organizations, this requires a shared language on how decisions are made. This language comes from the Performance Triangle (see Figure 13) and the management cycle, which together establish the elements and dimensions of agile.

CLARIFY YOUR CHOICES

Here are some things to consider when you commit to a specific choice:

- **Clarity is the result of high awareness and attention**: The key to clarity is non-judgemental awareness and feedback that enables learning.
- **Choice involves making a deliberate decision**: After the fact, it is easy to judge the quality of the decision.
- **The defining moment**: This is when utmost clarity leads to the obvious choice.
- **Interference**: Focusing on Self 2 is how you deal with interference.

Follow the steps in Tool #9, It's Your Choice, to clarify your choice for agile.

AMBIGUITY

Ambiguity requires flexibility and higher degrees of freedom (room to move). Ambiguity increases when markets develop or dissolve, industries transform, loyalties vanish, taboos get broken and boundaries blur. The challenge of high ambiguity in traditional organizations is that it can lead to people setting new rules and limiting boundaries. Managerial principles are the tools to cope with high ambiguity.

Choice involves making decisions about how to deal with ambiguity. The agile solution is to accept that people need to have choice, support them in their thinking so that they can assume responsibility, and give them what they need to move in one direction. The final stage of cementing choice in an organization is to explore how the system can facilitate people thinking at scale.

The choice shift: In times of increasing ambiguity, rules must enable choice. When the future is unclear, choice in decision-making performs better than standard operating procedures. Greater ambiguity is a frequent cause of 'infected' rules and the lack of discipline to follow them. Agility and speed in dealing with ambiguity require a design based on choice.

Choice in mentoring: The second phase of mentoring involves a moment of clarity and making a choice. It rests on the insights you have gained from the Agile Diagnostic (see Tool #4), the dimensions and elements you have identified, and the shared language you have established that lead to your choice of agile. The critical intervention points will guide your next phase.

As an executive, it's your choice: The inner game helps you to develop a clear strategy and clarify the long-term goals and direction of your organization. As there are always alternative opportunities and temptations, it is important to be clear about your own contribution. Make a deliberate choice to move in your direction. But be aware, as you always work with others, that you need to share and agree on one direction to build reliable relationships.

Before you do so, take time for your Choice Break on the next page.

MY CHOICE BREAK

 What are your challenges in making critical choices? Use Tool #9, It's Your Choice.

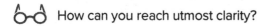 How can you reach utmost clarity?

How can you enable your organization to reach agreement and connect with others in order to move in one direction?

Nudge #5 provided an introduction to choice. Choice is about how you deal with ambiguity in your organization. Your next nudge is about trust.

CHOICE

Choice is the prerequisite for self-responsibility. It means leaving the choice to the performer and learner. It is the means by which your organization can deal with an ambiguous market context.

KEY SECTION IDEAS

- Choice is the precondition for self-responsibility in organizations
- Reaching the moment of clarity at scale is how organizations can enable choice
- A shared language helps you to reach clarity at scale throughout your organization
- Rules that facilitate choice are the means to deal with ambiguity
- The shift to people-centricity takes shape with your choice of agile

ACTION AGENDA

- Use Tool #9, It's Your Choice, to think about how you can reach clarity
- Use techniques relating to choice to bring agile into your organization

FURTHER READING

On self-responsibility: Sprenger, R. (2007). *Das Prinzip Selbstverantwortung: Wege zur Motivation*. Frankfurt a M: Campus.

TRUST

Trust is another part of the inner game. It is needed to mobilize resources in times of uncertainty. Nudge #6 explores the importance of trust and offers tools to help you review and develop trust. It further makes the case that trust is the key to uncertainty in organizations.

NUDGE #6: TRUST YOURSELF AND YOUR TEAM
Mobilize your resources to make agile your way.

"Trust becomes important when you let go of certain mental control. When Self 1 is in doubt, the flow is broken. Doubts lead to confusion and the paralysis of action. When you are focused, you are conscious of your purpose, fully engaged in the present, and the voice of Self 1 is not heard" (Gallwey, 2000). The more you trust Self 2, the less doubts and uncertainties will interfere with your performance and actions. Trust in Self 2 means that it's you that performs by engaging your full talent. But Self 2 cannot be controlled by conscious thought. It takes trust and humility to do this. Arrogance means thinking that we know everything. Trust in ourselves means acknowledging that we don't know everything. This makes us more aware and more able to learn. If we trust Self 2, it will take over control.

Uncertainty makes it difficult to turn opportunities into value. Risks are everywhere, but agility builds on trust. Step 3 of the management cycle, 'mobilize the energy' (see Section #3 of Chapter 2), ensures at scale throughout the organization that people are trusted and that there is trust in the abilities of collaborators to overcome uncertainties and capture value.

How do we mobilize resources? Trust is a prerequisite for self-organization. Leaders must have trust in teams that organize themselves. And teams must trust their own abilities in an uncertain context. Trust is the only way to cope with high uncertainty.

TRUST IS SPEED AND AGILITY

With trust, there is no need to wait for bureaucratic systems, such as objective agreements, to be modified to get things done. Trust directly reduces the time required to act and enhances flexibility. With trust, people exchange critical information that is essential for the survival of a business. To achieve speed and agility, leaders need to let go, trust and reduce control. Trust compensates for the impossible need to have everything under control: it makes us ready to let go and reduce control because we expect others to be competent and willing.

TRUST REDUCES COSTS

Trust is a control with low transaction costs. It works without the need for formal contractual agreements. If you need to reduce your operating costs, then look at your operating system and find areas that could be improved by adding more trust.

TRUST BUILDS COMMITMENT

Trust is a normal thing when dealing with people. Delegation depends on leaders who trust their employees to get the job done. There is nothing that creates more accountability than trust. Trust is a position with resistance and power. It is robust. Trust works better than any safety activity.

Trust in one's own inner resources (or the resources of others, if you are acting as a coach) is the essential link that puts things in motion. It is trust in a natural learning process. By avoiding corrective comments – 'do this, do that' – we trust the awareness and the dedicated choice of the learner, and improvement and learning take place. It requires trust in yourself, your skills and your potential, and trust in your coaching, to keep instructions back. Trusting your inner ability to learn may feel like you are losing control. The fact is that you are gaining control – self-control. A high degree of self-trust needs many tests of trust. To reduce control requires trust – letting go and encouraging employees to find their way. The roots of courage are self-trust. But courage needs to sit alongside respect for others.

UNCERTAINTY

Uncertainty challenges our strategy. The life cycle of strategies shortens, the results are less stable, dependencies on partners increase and transparency creates reputational risks. This all creates more uncertainty in our organizations. The challenge with uncertainty in traditional organizations is that it can lead to us telling people what to do and making decisions ourselves. Whom do we trust – people or systems? Leaders increase trust through positive interactions with employees.

Trust mobilizes resources in times of uncertainty. The agile solution is to build trust, support people to act and give them the resources they need to get things done. As such, we must explore the options for how managers can help people to collaborate. Then, we must identify and suggest implementation systems that mobilize energies at scale throughout the organization.

The trust shift: To cope with rising levels of uncertainty, leaders need to trust rather than command. The only way to deal with uncertainty is to trust in your own abilities. With increasing uncertainty, it is important to define a management policy that balances responsibility with outside control. The fix for flawed leadership is to design interactions better so as to improve relationships and support collaboration. To prevent creeping uncertainty from hampering performance, interactions require a design with features that enable trust.

Trust in mentoring: Learning is the third phase of mentoring; it is where your expertise helps you to transform and develop agile at scale. Trust in your own abilities and in the abilities of your team is essential in how you and your team collaborate to successfully make the shift.

As an executive, trust your abilities: The inner game helps you to translate strategy into action. The task is to mobilize your resources to get things done. You have all of the resources within your control. Hence, you know what you can rely on. Trust in your own ability and the abilities of others. Trust is the strongest bonding mechanism for collaboration.

Now take time for your Trust Break on the next page.

MY TRUST BREAK

 What are your challenges in building trust? Use Tool #10, Examine Trust, to test the trust in your organization and Tool #11, Review Commitment, to find out whether commitment creates value.

 How can you reach utmost trust?

 How can you enable your organization to trust and commit in mobilizing energy?

This section offered an introduction to trust as part of a chapter on the techniques of the inner game. Nudges #3 to #6 were all about the inner game. They encouraged you to think about what drives learning and performance. Your next nudge switches from techniques to resources.

TRUST

Trust is needed to mobilize resources in times of uncertainty.

KEY SECTION IDEAS

- Trust is a precondition for self-organization, and leadership depends on trust
- Trust improves speed and agility, reduces cost, and builds commitment
- Trust is the means to deal with uncertainty
- The shift to people-centricity needs learning – trust yourself and your team to learn and develop

ACTION AGENDA

- Take the Trust Break to think about trust in your team (use Tool #10, Examine Trust, and Tool #11, Review Commitment)
- Use trust to mobilize resources and shift to people-centricity in your organization

FURTHER READING

On trust: Sprenger, R. (2007). *Vertrauen führt: Worauf es in Unternehmen ankommt*. Frankfurt a M: Campus.

CHAPTER 4

Resources

The skilful application of the principles of the inner game is the prerequisite for people to effectively mobilize their resources and succeed with the challenges of their outer game. With Nudge #7, we will explore how focusing our attention, time and energy in combination offers a higher return on management. These are the critical resources that you need to keep in mind on your journey to agile and beyond.

NUDGE #7: RETURN ON MANAGEMENT
Mobilize your resources for agile.

The most talented people are able to use their resources most effectively and efficiently. They combine extraordinary motivation and the ability to improve quickly to release productive energy. Focus of attention is about the ability to learn, and time creates the momentum to turn motivation into energy.

Start to evaluate your resources with the following test:

	Fully disagree					+/-				Fully agree	
	0	10	20	30	40	50	60	70	80	90	100
I engage all my energy												
I use my time effectively												
I focus my attention												

Here is a simple formula (Simons and Davila, 1998) that can be used to explore how you use your resources:

$$\textit{Return on management} = \frac{\textit{Productive organizational energy released}}{\textit{Management time and attention invested}}$$

With your scores from the above test, use this formula and calculate your return on management. This is just to experience how the formula works.

Return on management is an imaginary score that indicates how well you use your resources: a score greater than 0.5 indicates that you are releasing productive energy in your organization with little time and attention invested. You are efficient and effective. A score of less than 0.5 means that your investment in time and attention do not release sufficient productive energy in your organization. You are inefficient and ineffective. Of course, the real world is more complex than the simple test suggests. The intent of the test was to get you to think about your resources.

The idea is to invest as little time and attention in management as possible while getting the most of the energy released. Time and energy are limited resources. Energy is a resource that requires refuelling.

Energy is the power that emerges when humans combine readiness, commitment and engagement. It is a limited resource with some stretch. Energy can only be redirected, not created or removed. But humans don't always have access to full energy. It needs to be renewed and refuelled when it has been used up. Refuelling is an investment that takes time. And the energy level cannot exceed 100% all of the time.

Focus of attention is a resource that is related to effectiveness. The human capacity for attention is also limited. The task is to concentrate on those things that offer the most value. The challenge is to reach a high level of focus and maintain it at that level. This mental process consumes a considerable amount of energy but it results in the release of productive energy. When attention and energy combine, they create flow (see Chapter 3).

Time is a resource that is commonly related to efficiency. Humans have a limited amount of time available. We cannot change time. Time is the only resource that cannot be enlarged, copied or stored. But how we invest our time, and whether we use it wisely, makes a difference. The challenge is to reach controlled momentum – when time and energy merge to create flow.

It is therefore clear that *focus of attention*, *time* and *energy* are the critical resources. Focus of attention is the willpower with which humans reach clarity. Time creates momentum, and energy is the power to perform and get things done.

Focus of attention, time and energy are interconnected. Think for a moment about the analogy with photography outlined in Figure 35.

	Photography	Outcomes
Attention	Lens, focal length	What gets attention: wide angle or telescopic
Time	Shutter speed	Exposure time: high or low Captures the moment at the right speed of motion
Energy	Aperture, light sensitivity	Depth of field, grain: high or low Quality: highlight important elements, sharpness, quality
Decision	Object, perspective, light	Clarity, the defining moment
Result	The image	Uniqueness

FIGURE 35: RESOURCES

Photographers have many options when they set out to capture the right image, select important parts of it and make sure the light adds the right atmosphere for a unique image. The lens and focal length determine what gets attention. The shutter speed determines exposure time and with it the ability to capture high-speed movement. Aperture and light sensitivity allow variations in the depth of field and grain. This determines what matters and the quality of the image – that is, its energy. In that sense, there are similarities between photography and management.

Managing focus of attention, time and energy is an individual responsibility. But it is the responsibility of the leader and the organization to establish a work environment where people provide a high return but at the same time take care of their resources.

Does your organization have a high return on management? There are friends and foes of this concept (adapted from Simons and Davila, 1998). Friends of a high return on management include the following:

- Utmost clarity exists about which clients, projects, investments and activities are out of bounds

- Your critical performance variables are driven by a healthy fear of failure
- Your managers can recall their metrics (and there are never more than seven)
- Paperwork and processes exist only where they help you to do good work
- Employees know what keeps the boss up at 3am, and that's what they focus on in their work – all day long

And the foes of a high return on management include as follows:
- Your organization has a 'sky is the limit' strategy with a vague mission
- Your critical performance measures are politically correct: they involve all stakeholders and don't threaten anyone
- Employees are unsure about their accountability, or there is so much time available to them that it is hard to focus
- Planning, budgeting and controls have taken over
- Employees have little awareness of the priorities of the organization

In light of this overview of return on management, take the Resource Break on the next page to think about your resources. Then continue with Nudge #8 to review your productive energy.

MY RESOURCE BREAK

 What challenges do you face relating to your resources?

 What is your return on management?

 What are the things you do to achieve a high return on management?

MY RESOURCES

Focus of attention, *time* and *energy* are the critical resources.

KEY SECTION IDEAS

- Attention, time and energy are limited
- Time is about efficiency – it cannot be enlarged, copied or stored
- Attention is related to effectiveness – it requires mental effort to focus attention and reach clarity
- Energy needs to be refuelled if it is to release its power over a long time period

ACTION AGENDA

- Review your return on management with the Resource Break
- Identify the friends and foes of your return on management

FURTHER READING

On return on management: Simons, R. and Davila, A. (1998). How high is your return on management? *Harvard Business Review*, January–February. Accessed 23 April 2020. https://hbr.org/1998/01/how-high-is-your-return-on-management.

ENERGY

Building on the above overview of the elements that make up a high return on management, Nudge #8 dives into energy – the element that offers productivity and power through high readiness, engagement and activity.

NUDGE #8: POWER UP YOUR ENERGY
Balance engagement and refuelling to succeed on your way to agile.

Physics tells us that, in general, the sum of all energies is constant – it can only be redirected. With humans, energy is a limited resource with some stretch. It needs to be renewed and refuelled when it has been used up. Refuelling is an investment that takes time. Exceeding 100% energy capacity for a long time period has consequences. And, humans don't always have full access to their energy.

ENERGY FOLLOWS ATTENTION

Energy flows to where there is attention. If we focus our energy and attention on habitual emotions and events that occurred in to past, we reduce the energy available in the present. Equally, a focus on the external, material world limits the amount of energy available to our inner world, which consists of the thoughts and feelings required to create new things.

If we bring our attention and energy to the present, over time, our mind gives in and we reach a creative state. We switch from the physical to the quantum world (see Chapter 3): we are in the here and now, and we have access to all possibilities.

The quantum world consists of invisible energy and information. It is the field of intelligence and awareness beyond space and time. Awareness establishes consciousness of energy through attention and observation. Awareness combines with higher-frequency information. That's the quantum world with all its possibilities. When the observer searches for the material world, energy and information collapse (i.e. the quantum effect), and energy and information return to matter.

EMOTIONS ARE ENERGY

Emotions are linked to people, places and things. They are the feedback we receive from our experiences. Our senses record external information, and neurons connect this information to make patterns. Our memory is a snapshot of our experiences. As soon as we withdraw our attention from emotions (the positive and negative), energy is set free. As such, we gain sufficient energy to create new things.

CHANGING ENERGY

Clear intentions and elevated emotions are needed to change energy. This happens in defining moments when people have access to all possibilities. How can we access the human potential? Intentions are thoughts with an electrical charge; they come with high energy and high frequency and they carry information. Emotions consist of energy with a magnetic charge. In the quantum environment, potential is frequency with information. If my energy frequency fits the frequency of my potential, then this attracts new experience. It will find you. With clear intentions and higher emotions, awareness attracts new experience. This is very handy. To attract new experience, we just need to pay attention and be aware.

INDIVIDUAL ENERGY

Energy requires that work is purposeful and that it personally matters to us. It enables flow – the state of peak performance. Here are some practical things to think about your personal energy and how to keep it a high levels:

- **Body – the physical energy**: a good physical condition is a prerequisite for achieving peak performance levels
- **Mind/feeling – the quality of the energy**: positive energy leads to higher performance, while negative energy reduces performance. The task is to establish rituals that mobilize the positive energy: breathing, stories and purpose
- **Head/attitude – the focus of energy**: interference limits our focus and is expensive – think of multitasking, emails and telephone calls
- **Spirit – the energy behind purpose and meaning**: performance is the result of daily activities that are consistent with our values, and this offers purpose and meaning.

ORGANIZATIONAL ENERGY

Energy can be compared with culture in organizations. For organizations to tackle higher challenges, it is important that there is minimum interference from within – they must have a culture that is free from viruses. The task is to establish a work environment that releases the productive energies of its people. A productive corporate culture has a positive impact on success. This is how productive energy unfolds.

A vibrant culture releases the productive energy of people. Energy the momentum. I define energy as the outcome of collective attention and productive use of time. It is a powerful space between accumulated capabilities and resources directed towards the purpose of an organization.

High energy means that all resources are dedicated towards maximizing the capabilities of an organization and building competitive advantage. In a vibrant culture, all resources collaborate to release productive energy.

Physics teaches that the sum of all energy remains constant. Energy does not appear from nowhere, nor does it disappear anywhere. Energy can only be transformed. Energy is a process, not a thing. It can only be redirected or used differently. For example, when people release their energy and do things out of passion, then this result in an equal amount of joy and fulfilment.

A vibrant culture with high energy supports overall alignment in an organization. Resources commit to this shared foundation, which means that they naturally align with the goals of the organization.

Many organizations develop capabilities, knowledge and skills. But they are blind when it comes to capacity and energy. Individuals, teams and organizations can easily enhance their capacity with few interventions. The task is to align the available energies in the best possible way. Feng shui, a Chinese art, does exactly that: it directs all energies in the right direction.

Now take your Energy Break (on the next page) to think about your energy and the energy in your organization.

MY ENERGY BREAK

 What challenges do you face with your energy? Use Tool #12, Check Your Energy, to review where you are with your energy, and then use Tool #13, Refuel Your Energy, to identify your energy strategy.

 What is your energy level? Why?

 What can you do to release more productive energy?

This nudge offered the fundamentals of energy. Next with Nudge #9, we look at focus of attention as a key resource.

ENERGY

Energy is the power that emerges when humans combine readiness, commitment and engagement.

KEY SECTION IDEAS

- Energy is a limited resource with some stretch
- Energy needs to be refuelled when it has been used up

ACTION AGENDA

- Take the Energy Break: How can you release more productive energy?
- Check your energy level by using Tool #12, Check Your Energy
- Find ways to refuel and renew your energy by using Tool #13, Refuel Your Energy

FURTHER READING

On individual energy: Schwartz T. and McCarthy, C. (2007). Manage your energy, not your time. *Harvard Business Review*, October. Accessed 23 April 2020. https://hbr.org/2007/10/manage-your-energy-not-your-time.

On organizational energy: Bruch, H. and Ghoshal, S. (2004). *A Bias for Action: How Effective Managers Harness Their Willpower, Achieve Results, and Stop Wasting Time*. Boston: Harvard Business School Press.

FOCUS OF ATTENTION

Focus is part of the inner game and the second resource that determines your return on management. It involves paying attention, concentrating so as to focus on the things that matter to us, and learning quickly. Nudge #9 explores a very valuable resource that we as humans have available for any activity that requires our mind to be active.

This limited resource is attention. Focus is self-initiated attention to what matters most. It is a conscious act of concentration that requires energy. The challenge for people is to maintain focus over a period of time. Managers have a choice between self-initiated focus of attention and goal achievement following detailed performance targets.

NUDGE #9: FOCUS YOUR ATTENTION
Learn to perform with your choice of agile.

By focusing our attention we make contact with everything in the world, and by that means alone things become knowable and understandable to us. Attention is critical to learning, understanding and proficiency of action. Only when we pay full attention do we engage all our resources so as to be effective. When we give our full attention, our self-produced interference is neutralized. With full attention, there is no room for Self 1 (see Chapter 3).

Focus is energy channelled towards a specific outcome. Focused managers can concentrate despite the many distractions that come up every day. Rather than just react to a specific interference, focus helps us to stay on track and pursue our goals. Our activities are directed towards a specific purpose. Focused behaviour does not emerge by chance. It is a deliberate mental act and follows personal discipline.

Focus of attention is a quantum environment. At the moment of observation, new insights are created, which leads to new knowledge. Deliberate attention mobilizes behaviours and thoughts.

Our brain has a limited capacity to process information. Focus involves selection of what information gets attention and what needs to be ignored. Information that does not get attention within seconds is lost.

Focus means paying attention to things that matter. Attention is mental presence. Focus is the filter that separates important from unimportant information. It separates new information and information that creates emotions from other information. Information that is loaded with emotions directs attention more easily than other types of information. Needs, interests, mindsets and motives are important for how attention emerges and how it separates out information.

Attention is linked to awareness. When we pay attention to information, we become aware. But our brain also processes information that does not receive our attention. This attention happens unconsciously. While paying attention is an unconscious brain activity, we can influence what gets our attention as a controlled process. This concentrated attention, however, differs in its duration, intensity and depth.

Attention always deals with the topic that has highest priority. The priority itself is triggered by a deviation from the normal, and error or something that is desirable.

It is impossible to simultaneously (i.e. in the same millisecond) pay attention to different triggers – for example, an optical or tacit. This means that attention can be focused on one thing only. Switching attention from one thing to another requires energy, and it can make us tired quickly.

If we pay attention to something particular, it becomes a habit. That's why it makes sense to review what gets our attention from time to time.

Returning to the business world: volatility makes it hard to stay on track and follow our chosen path, whereas agility helps us to remain flexible and stay on track. Step 4 of the management cycle, 'maintain the focus' (see Section #3 of Chapter 2), ensures that people have the means to deliver value even when things change frequently and rapidly at scale throughout their organization.

How do we maintain the focus? As focus of attention is an essential skill in learning, attentive and focused people are better at dealing with fast-changing environments.

At work, focus is likely the most important component of superior performance in every activity and at every level of sophistication. As Peter M. Senge (1999) reinforced, "Paying attention is not a trivial task. Indeed, much of the process of mastering any domain involves continual refinement in the capacity to pay attention, while simultaneously performing. I believe all organizations must develop their own practices and disciplines for cultivating attentiveness." Focus brings clarity to whatever we observe. It is governed by our choice and desire. And it takes trust to rely on unconscious control.

Focus is power: CEOs are constantly confronted with a barrage of decisions and actions. Multitasking can be appropriate for highly automated tasks to a degree, but for high-stakes decisions it just doesn't work. The frontal part of the brain uses the most energy and is what you use for new, complex decisions. So, you have to shunt as much energy as possible to that part. You do that by focusing your thinking and by limiting outside sensory input. Many of us have forgotten how to get to this high level of focus quickly, and this problem becomes particularly relevant when it applies to group of people, let alone whole organizations. Organizations need management techniques to help their people focus their attention.

Focus means goal orientation: It involves concentration on a specific thing without being distracted. It requires people to deliberately direct their activities towards their goal. Focus is a conscious act that requires energy. As such, it is a distinct skill to follow your intentions and remain focused over a long period of time.

A word of caution: too much focus makes people blind to other opportunities. The good news is that focus requires energy, meaning that high levels of focus are naturally complemented by routine-type work that allows energy to be refuelled. People use relaxing moments to ensure that they can refocus on relevant things.

Focus of attention has a huge benefit for the leadership in organization. It builds on goal orientation without the negative effects of management by objectives. As I have argued extensively (Michel, 2013, 2017), goals and target-setting mechanisms have a negative effect on people's performance. But focus of attention uses critical performance variables – the measurement component of objectives – as observation points. As such, people rely on those metrics that are relevant to their work. Responsible people know the difference between good performance and bad performance. There is no need to complement critical performance variables with standards. In fact, setting standards or targets for metrics eliminates the entire effect of the focus of attention. It undermines the inner game.

VOLATILITY

Dynamic environments are now the norm. Speed, connective technologies and real-time processes are increasing the need for quick decisions. Today, people always expect an immediate response. The challenge in this environment of high volatility is that when control fails, we tend to install more of it, and our default behaviour is to keep everything under control. Controls are the leadership tools traditionally used to cope with the dynamics of the environment.

In the agile approach, focus of attention is the technique by which people learn to perform in a volatile environment. The solution comes from focus of attention: how people *engage and adhere* to maintain the chosen direction.

The focus shift: To address greater volatility, tools must focus attention rather than aim. When things change quickly, people need something they can hold on to. Use tools that focus attention on what is important. With increasing volatility and market dynamics, it is important to get your organization's policy on control right and to achieve a balance between enabling self-initiative and fostering goal achievement. The way to fix unhelpful tools is to redesign them to focus on purpose and collaboration. Prevent focus on the wrong things by using tools that help people to focus their attention rather than just enabling control.

Focus attention through mentoring: Attention is part of the first and second phases of mentoring (see Section #5 of Chapter 2). Diagnostic insights offer observation points. By focusing on the critical issues, our mind starts to learn and find solutions to the issues at hand.

As an executive, focus your attention: Attention is a limited resource and it requires energy to maintain it. Hence, it is important not to get distracted from maintaining a high level of energy. Also think about your 'stop' time and how you refuel your energy. Boundaries and beliefs (Michel, 2013) guide your attention span. Focus ensures that you will reach your destination – that you will be able to meet the challenges that you have set out.

FOCUS AND ENERGY

High focus releases productive energy. Awareness creates clarity. Focus maintains attention. In combination, these key elements lead to the high return on management that is needed to operate in a complex and volatile context.

Four modes – effective, disconnected, frantic and paralysed (Figure 36) – can be used to identify how your focus leads to energy. Achieving effectiveness comes about from the ability to pay attention, concentrate in order to focus, and quickly learn to get to the flow zone and stay there.

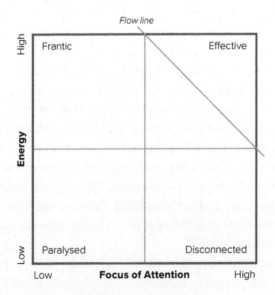

FIGURE 36: FOCUS AND ENERGY

The effective: High focus, high energy. Clarity leads to flow. Ten per cent of leaders fall into this category. They:
- Use experience, stand back and reflect
- Are self-responsible, deliberate and aware
- Wish to contribute something important

The disconnected: High focus, low energy. Lots of thinking with little impact. Forty per cent of leaders fall into this category. They:
- Confuse ideas with outcomes
- Allow short-term thinking to lead them in faulty directions
- Allow their habits to dominate, with changing topics

The frantic: Low focus, high energy. Lots of headless action. Twenty per cent of leaders fall into this category. They:
- Confuse busy engagement with productive solutions
- Defend themselves with power mechanisms
- Destroy energy and lack personal resources

The paralysed: Low focus, low energy. Little action and ambition. Thirty per cent of leaders fall into this category. They:
- Administrate and follow others
- Show little initiative and hardly change
- Are always busy and have an explanation for everything

Strategies for reaching the flow zone of high effectiveness include being aware, knowing with clarity, maintaining the focus, taking care of your energy and continuously learning. The solution involves the following:
- **Strengthen your awareness, focus your attention and preserve your energy**
- **Remove organizational interference**: fix faulty leadership and the virus-infected culture (the fix with agile features)

Now, take the Focus Break to sharpen your attention.

Be aware: focus of attention requires skill and training to get there. To get the full experience of the power of focus of attention, it is helpful to use the guidance of an expert who offers practical exercises on how to learn to use focus of attention in the most effective way.

MY FOCUS BREAK

 What challenges do you face with your focus? Use Tool #14, Pay Attention, to review the themes that require your attention.

 What are your ways of paying attention? Why?

How can you focus attention to release more productive energy?

Nudge #9 provided an introduction to focus of attention. This is the resource and technique that helps us to learn and perform. Awareness and concentration through focus are also a means to deal with higher volatility and complexity. Your next nudge is about time.

FOCUS OF ATTENTION

Focus of attention is concentrated mental capacity on things that matter to us.

KEY SECTION IDEAS

- Focus of attention is a limited resource
- Focus of attention is the resource that deals with volatility
- Four modes can be used to identify your focus of attention and strategies for achieving flow
- Focus of attention triggers learning and performance
- The shift to people-centricity replaces detailed performance targets with the skill of focusing attention

ACTION AGENDA

- Identify your focus mode and strategy in order to reach the flow zone
- Use the Focus Break to think about how to focus and release more energy
- Use Tool #14, Pay Attention, to identify your attention priorities

FURTHER READING

On individual attention: Gallwey, W. T. (2000). *The Inner Game of Work*. New York: Random House.

On organizational attention: Simons, R. (1995). *Levers of Control: How Managers Use Innovative Control Systems to Drive Strategic Renewal*. Boston: Harvard Business School Press.

TIME

Time is the third element that determines a high return on management. It is the resource that we commonly relate to efficiency. Nudge #10 explores the investments you can make into your pace to achieve and maintain a high momentum that releases productive energies. Time is a source of energy.

Humans have a limited amount of time available. We cannot change time – it continuously flows. Time is limited. But how we invest our time, and whether we use it wisely, makes a difference. As time itself cannot be managed, you must decide how to use time. 'Time management' is a misnomer. The challenge is to reach a high momentum – when time and energy merge to create flow. But momentum is like a race car without brakes. It needs to be controlled.

NUDGE #10: MAINTAIN THE MOMENTUM
Keep the pace on your journey to agile.

Time has the same value as money. Therefore, before you continue reading, take time to account of your time. To get this started, use Tool #15, Time Accounts, to review your time drivers. Do you spend your time in line with your needs and your role?

For most activities at work, time is a critical factor. Most of the time, time manages us – not the other way around. We can be smart about what we do within a given time frame. It is, therefore, important that you create awareness of your time: the relationship between time and your activities. Before digging into your time, consider Tool #16, 101 on Executive Time.

WHAT IS TIME?

Space and time belong to the foundations of human awareness and thinking. We are less aware of time than of space. Try this experiment: find an old alarm clock that ticks and set it to three minutes. Observe how time passes without looking at the clock. How did you experience your three minutes? Could you sense time? In the present? As an extension of the past and future? As a limit? As stress? As fulfilment?

Here is an overview of different aspects of time:

- **Physical aspects of time**: Aristoteles defined time as a number of motions. Galileo saw time as an independent variable. Newton defined absolute time as something that continuously flows without interference from other things. Einstein corrected that idea with the introduction of relativity theory, in which time is a relative term that is connected with space as the fourth dimension.
- **Biological aspects of time**: The focus here is on time awareness and temporal rhythms with endogenous 'zeitgeber' (cues), such as our inner clock, and exogenous zeitgeber, such as light and temperature.
- **Psychological aspects of time**: The focus here is on how we perceive time, how it influences behaviours, and our orientation with instances in time.
- **Philosophical aspects of time**: Time is seen as the opposite of eternity. For Augustine, time was a phenomenon within God's creation. For God, everything is present time. For Kant, time was a human capacity to experience time as flow and a sequence of instances. Insights are dependent on time and space. Hegel related time to spirit. The present includes the past and the future. Every historical moment is a movement in time and space. Time shapes insights and worldviews. Heidegger related time to timeliness, finiteness and limitation in a positive sense, and this requires us to pick our opportunities.

TIME AND ENERGY

High momentum releases productive energy. Trust is the fastest management concept. With no other management connect, leaders get things done equally fast. Choice removes doubt and speeds up decisions. In combination, these key elements contribute to the high return on management that is needed to operate in an ambiguous and uncertain context.

Four modes – efficient, fruitless, hyper and inactive (Figure 37) – can be used to identify how the correct use of time leads to energy. Using time effectively involves using momentum, action and motivation to get into the flow zone and stay there.

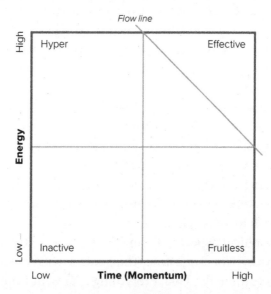

FIGURE 37: TIME AND ENERGY

The efficient: High momentum, high energy. Trust and choice lead to flow. Ten per cent of leaders fall into this category. They:
- Use experience, decide and act
- Are motivated, have choice and have trust
- Want to do something important

The fruitless: High momentum, low energy. Control limits speed. Forty per cent of leaders fall into this category. They:
- Confuse action with impact

- Use short-term reactions to create uncertainty
- Follow rules and interact to irritate

The hyper: Low momentum, high energy. Speed is out of control. Twenty per cent of leaders fall into this category. They:
- Confuse being busy with productive action
- Interfere through drama and mistrust
- Destroy energy but have no time

The inactive: Low momentum, low energy. Thirty per cent of leaders fall into this category. They:
- Work according to the rules and no more
- Wait for motivation to get things done
- Follow orders and resist change

Strategies for reaching the flow zone of high efficiency include moving in one direction, mobilizing the energy, and creating momentum, action and motivation. The solution involves the following:
- **Allow for choice and trust your capabilities and those of your team**
- **Remove organizational interference**: fix erroneous systems and a virus-infected culture (the fix has agile features)

EXECUTIVE PACE

Time is a source of energy that requires your careful investment. Following are a few things to consider in relation to time (use Tool #18, Executive Pace, to work through your time):
- Use the power of the past, present and future rather than traditional time management
- Use time as a continuum rather than discontinuity. It's the mindset that gets you into flow and peak performance
- View time as subjective and elastic rather than fixed and constant. Learn to speed up, slow down and stop
- Consider that people, your organization and your clients all have their own rhythms. You can adapt to them or shape them

- View time either as a clock or as a source of opportunities and creativity
- Use time as enjoyable source of energy

Organizational pace is a rhythm that follows a deliberate cycle with routines that guide executive pace.

In this light, use the Time Break below to reflect on your use of time.

MY TIME BREAK

 What challenges do you experience with your time? Use Tool #17, Pace Your Time, and Tool #18, Executive Pace.

 How do you pace yourself in time? Why?

⊕ How can you use time to release more productive energy?

Nudge #10 was about time and the need for discipline and efficiency. The next nudge is about space and accountability.

TIME

Time consists of moments and momentum that release productive energy.

KEY SECTION IDEAS

- Time is a limited resource. It cannot be changed. It continuously flows. Time and energy combine to create momentum

ACTION AGENDA

- Identify your time mode and strategies you can use to reach the flow zone
- Use Tool #15, Time Accounts, to identify the priorities with your time
- Use Tool #16, 101 on Executive Time, to reflect on your use of time
- Use the Time Beak to think about how you use time to release productive energy with Tool #17, Pace Your Time, and Tool #18, Executive Pace

FURTHER READING

On the meaning of time: Clemens, J. K. and Dalrymple, S. (2005). *Time Mastery: How Temporal Intelligence Will Make You a Stronger Leader*. New York: Amacon.

On time management: Mankins, M. (2004). Stop wasting valuable time. *Harvard Business Review*, September. Accessed 23 April 2020. https://hbr.org/2004/09/stop-wasting-valuable-time.

SPACE

'Give me some space' is what we say when something narrows our space or something important is ahead of us that requires reflection and action. Space is our fourth resource, and it is both individual and organizational. Energy, focus of attention and time happen in space. Accountability defines your management space and triggers organizational structure. With the help of accountability levers, Nudge #11 frames your specific space in time based on people-centric principles.

NUDGE #11: CREATE YOUR SPACE
Establish your accountability profile.

Before you frame your individual space, it is worthwhile to recognize the differences between the material and quantum environments along the space and time dimensions. The comparison shows why awareness through non-judgemental observation helps us to open up to agile – to new ways of looking at our world without fixating on our past experiences.

SPACE AND TIME

Space and time frame our material world with known people, objects, places and moments. We sense our environment as form, structure, mass and density. We cannot experience our material world fully without all of our senses. If one of the senses is missing, we perceive our reality differently. For example, skiing without visibility immediately creates uncertainty. Space, in the material world, is nearly unlimited – eternal.

Moving from one place to another takes time. Newton explained that we experience time through movement: it takes time to get from Awareness Point 1 to Awareness Point 2.

Interactions with the environment are what make us who we are as humans. Experiences from the past create patterns in our memory. With a focus on the material world, the three-dimensional, known and predictable environment takes over. Fixed thoughts, behaviours and actions are the result.

Managers experience space and time through their actions: who does what when?

TIME AND SPACE

Time and space make up the non-physical quantum environment, an inverse world with unknowns, infinite possibilities and energy. There is more time than space. Time is infinite, eternity, timeless. Attention and focus are timeless. The self diverts attention from the outside to the self to access time and space. With this, attention is on space, energy, frequency and information.

Accessing quantum energy requires a change from a closed focus (material) to an open focus: a change from beta state to alpha (see Chapter 3). Mind and matter are united as energy – waves with a specific frequency that are accessible through awareness. This opens us up to multiple spaces with infinite possibilities.

Through observation, energy electrons appear as matter. This translates the unknown into the known. If the observation stops, the electron turns back into energy. Non-judgemental observation is the practical application that we use with the inner game to open the focus.

Managers experience time and space when they experience utmost clarity or flow: peak performance is the result.

Accountability is personal space. Agile is based on self-responsibility with the choice to focus on Self 2. Assuming responsibility creates accountability – within space and time. As such, accountability defines your space. It therefore makes sense to use a practical tool to help you define your accountability in an agile context. Rather than fixed rights and duties, agile looks at accountability as a space that you can shape, move in and maintain to meet your needs.

Robert Simons (2005), in his seminal book *Levers of Organization Design*, proposes an elegant way to create your space with four levers: span of control, span of accountability, span of influence and span of support. Figure 38 combines these levers into the management space. A small span means little space. A wide span means lots of space.

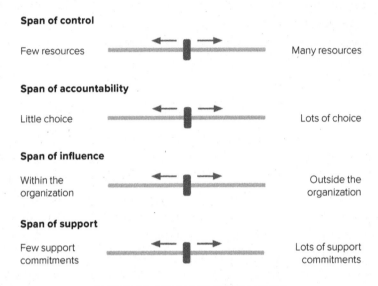

Span of control

Few resources ⟵ ▮ ⟶ Many resources

Span of accountability

Little choice ⟵ ▮ ⟶ Lots of choice

Span of influence

Within the organization ⟵ ▮ ⟶ Outside the organization

Span of support

Few support commitments ⟵ ▮ ⟶ Lots of support commitments

FIGURE 38: ACCOUNTABILITY LEVERS

Span of control defines the resources you have available under your control. It includes balance sheet assets as well as intangible resources and people. Span of accountability defines the critical performance measures you have available, which may be few or many. Few metrics allow for a wide span of accountability. Many metrics narrow your space of accountability. Span of influence defines the interactions you have within your organization and with others outside your organization. Span of support defines collaboration, with little or lots of support from others.

Span of control and span of support represent the supply of organizational resources. Span of control defines the formal resources directly controlled by individuals: decision rights, facilities, information, and other tangible and intangible resources. Soft resources, such as support, are important for the functioning of complex organizations. The important question here is: what resources can I rely on?

Span of accountability and span of influence represent individuals' demand for resources. The degree of accountability defines the trade-offs between critical performance measures and incentives. It creates demand among individuals for the resources they need to achieve their goals, such as access to people, knowledge, facilities, information, infrastructure and the like. Demand is also created by pressures such as networks, outside resources or stretched goals. The important question here is: Whom do I need to interact with and influence to achieve my goals?

Executive space is defined by these spans:

- **Control**: What are the resources I can control to accomplish my tasks?
- **Accountability**: What measures can I use to evaluate my performance?
- **Influence**: Whom do I need to interact with and influence to achieve my goals?
- **Support**: How much support can I expect when I reach out to others for help?

Figure 39 combines the spans into a protocol that frames accountability as a space. It has been completed with an example relating to the accountability of a CEO. Tool #19 contains a blank version of the Accountability Profile for you to complete.

JOB: CEO	
POSITION	**ACCOUNTABILITY**
Responsibility: for the strategy and results of the organization **Reports to**: the board **Control**: management team **Resources**: organization, balance sheet, business functions, support staff, joint ventures, partnerships	**Metrics and results**: growth, earnings, share price, corporate health **Tasks**: strategy, risks, reputation, talent, systems, coordination **Rights**: leads the management board, decides on strategy, reputation, talent, systems, governance, support
COLLABORATION	**PROFILE**
Influence: decisions of the management team **Duties**: informs the board, informs the organization **Support for**: management team **Supported by**: the board	**Span of control** Few resources — Many resources **Span of accountability** Little choice — Lots of choice **Span of influence** Within the organization — Outside the organization **Span of support** Few support commitments — Lots of support commitments

FIGURE 39: ACCOUNTABILITY PROFILE

Equilibrium is needed between costly, in-demand resources and the supply of resources. The presence of equilibrium is determined via the X test (see the links between the spans in Figure 39). When the two lines cross, the resources are balanced in the space of the specific job.

Structure and accountability define organizational space and determine the demand and use of organizational resources. By aligning the spans, executives design their accountability in line with the needs of higher agility. In this way, accountability can be designed for the benefit of teams, functions and departments – essentially every talent in the organization. As such, structure emerges based on people-centric principles. Individual space integrates accountability into the workplace. In this way, the design of the workplace gains high importance.

Taking into account the CEO example in Figure 39, it is time to use the Space Break on the next page to define your accountability.

MY SPACE BREAK

 What challenges do you experience with your space?

 How do you use your space?

 How can you use space to create accountability?

Nudge #11 explored space as a means to clarify accountability. Accountability combines individual and organizational resources. The next nudge is about leadership everywhere and how it can be made to work for everyone in the organization.

SPACE

Space defines accountability and is a prerequisite for agile workplaces and structures.

KEY SECTION IDEAS

- Organizational space consists of matter and structure
- Structure follows accountability
- Individual space is closely linked to accountability and combines the material and quantum environments
- Accountability and non-judgemental observation enable executives to translate the unknown into the known, material world
- For people, space means workplace – it needs the right design

ACTION AGENDA

- Use the Space Break to think about your space and accountability
- Use Tool #19, Accountability Profile, to identify your space by describing your accountability

FURTHER READING

On accountability levers: Simons, R. (2005). *Levers of Organization Design: How Managers Use Accountability Systems for Greater Performance and Commitment.* Boston: Harvard Business School Press.

CHAPTER 5

Decisions

In previous chapters, we introduced the power of the inner game and discussed the resources every human being has available to learn and perform. These are the critical elements that make up an agile executive. In Chapter 2, "Five Leadership Dimensions," we explored the organizational environment executives need to unlock their talents and create value. Decisions are moments when the true nature of agile can be seen. They are when individual agility meets corporate agility. In the knowledge era, all people are executives. They make decisions. Nudge #12 is about decision-making and the opportunity to establish leadership everywhere.

NUDGE #12: ESTABLISH LEADERSHIP EVERYWHERE
Developing decision-making everywhere
is *the* competitive advantage.

Knowledge work is decision-making that uses the following process: understand, think, decide, act, engage and adhere. Traditional decision-making separates the thinking from the doing. The thinking resides with leaders at the top and the doing with people at the client front. Agile decision-making relies on the inner game and individual resources. Agile comes with the capacity to focus on potential and limit interference. Most interference in decision-making stems from systems that are inadequate in their support of executive decision-making. These systems were built on the traditional, negative assumptions about people.

Decision-making theory and social information processing theory distinguish between rational and heuristic reasoning. Rational reasoning is about thinking and acting in a manner that leads to an optimal result based on a person's values and risk preferences. Heuristic reasoning uses existing knowledge as a means to determine choices and behaviours. Self-interest and rational reasoning mutually influence each other. Self-interest asks for rational judgement when personal stakes are high. Then, individuals tend to apply more effort and rigour to their decisions.

For leaders, the challenge is to ensure that people can use their full potential and put it to the purpose of the customer. Many studies indicate that in order to achieve control, it may not be necessary to monitor employees closely. The general agreement is that managers should allow employees a degree of autonomy in determining goals and how best to achieve them. Because we want to get the best from employees, we need to take a closer look at the current practice in organizations to explore what a productive operating environment looks like.

PRODUCTIVE OPERATING ENVIRONMENTS

UNDERSTAND AND THINK

People's thoughts, ideas and creativity (often called social innovation) are positively related to organizational performance. But, for people's creativity to flourish, an environment is required that is open to new areas, cooperation, surprise, uncertainty and challenges.

Knowledge people have a set of inner maps. They use them as mental models to make sense of situations and help them make decisions. Such mental models are critical in knowledge-based work. They are deeply anchored, internal pictures of how the world works and they consist of the values that fundamentally determine our thoughts, decisions, actions and behaviours. Mental models allow us to take shortcuts and process information very quickly. With increasing experience, we add information to our maps, and as a consequence they change. This helps us to learn and find new solutions.

But too often, our thinking remains within the scope of what we are familiar with. It is worthwhile to share thoughts with others to expand our learning. The benefit for organizations not only comes from individual thinking but from collective minds. More people see different things. They can help each other to think outside the box and find improved solutions. The challenge is that collective thinking demands the alignment of our mental maps. It requires intense interaction and sharing of our beliefs, thoughts and assumptions.

CEOs need to be aware that their mental models travel fast. As with leadership style, people watch and amplify the leader's thinking. This means that the leader's thinking becomes dominant and can quickly reinforce positive or negative trends. Leaders' thoughts can seek out good ideas or block irrelevant things to strengthen the desired path.

In the industrial age, thinking was believed to remain at the top. Executives were employed to do the thinking. The thinking was clearly separated from the doing, which meant that it was the employees' task to implement decisions that had been taken by executives at the top. But fully benefitting from people's knowledge and skills requires delegating decision-making and making people accountable to simultaneously implement their decisions.

DECIDE

In knowledge-driven companies, people make decisions. Most decisions require a choice between conflicting goals. By definition, contradictory goals need a decision to be made. Conflicts cannot be solved in any other way. As such, decisions require a person that decides. And who decides becomes liable. Resolving conflicting goals is what makes an executive. As Peter F. Drucker (1967) said, in the knowledge age, employees have become executives. They make decisions.

The challenge for corporate leadership is to guide the decision-making in an organization. What will help your leaders and managers to decide between competing goals? In general, the organization's vision provides a long-term perspective that can be used to determine the decision content (what). Values help with the decision-making process (how). As guidelines, vision and values should create a lack of ambiguity. But values are by nature ambiguous.

When we claim 'transparency', we also include 'secrecy': we make the case for transparency as a value because some things need to be secret, otherwise there would be no reason to have such a value. But complexity cannot be reduced to A or B. Explicit values are needed to reduce bipolarity. This shows that defining values and vision is difficult and requires the utmost care. As a rule of thumb, some 'non-transparency' helps with values. And problems with values are usually related to too much precision – for example, detailed descriptions of each value with full transparency. Detailed values will always get stuck in situations where they cannot be followed as articulated. More detail calls for more situations where the values are the default. This results in a loss of credibility of the values and the leaders who put them in place.

ACT

Performance is the result of action, not intent. People put their energy into things they care about. And energy requires that action is meaningful. It also implies that people are responsible – for example, they take the initiative and get things done. Taking action needs choice, self-control and determination. Allowing people to take responsibility attracts the best talent to an organization, because they can live their own goals.

The effectiveness of objective agreements as a means to achieve goal-directed behaviour depends on markets. Goals are a bargaining topic. The context of Drucker's idea on goal orientation was the plan economy. But the working environment has fundamentally changed. And unfortunately, over time Drucker's tool became perverted in many organizations, which turned it into a means of control. The value of action comes from bundled energy, not making money. Hence, be careful with the use of objective agreements. Employees perceive seismographic signals, and a well-intended idea might turn against you.

ENGAGE AND ADHERE

Values determine our behaviours. They work well in normal times. However, in situations of conflict, our oldest and most dominant behaviour stake charge – they are hardened through time in our brain. And when things go wrong, we are always quick in pointing to the guilty individual. The logic goes, 'because things went wrong and there is a guilty person, we need to fix the person to prevent repeat non-performance.' Organizations invest huge amounts in fixing people. The 'repair intelligence' of organizations is high but rather ineffective. To fix these hardwired behaviours, organizations conduct training; this is commonly referred to as 'learning' but it is really about changing their conduct. We tell people what to do or what not to do rather than call for them to use their creativity, ideas and knowledge to get things right.

Learning is always done in anticipation of our own performance. Self-change works as Johann Wolfgang von Goethe observed: "All change results from sorrow." Getting out of a situation only happens through suffering. Moreover, we cannot induce fear in people to get things done. The most effective learning takes place when people are responsible for their own behaviours and results. It is that simple.

Executives make 20 decision per day – some big, some small. In an agile and enabling environment, every employee executive makes ten decisions per day – some important, others less so. In an organization of 500 executives, this results in 5,000 decisions per day. In a year, this amounts to almost two million decisions.

We invest huge amounts of money in the design of new products, quality processes, and change and incentive plans. And in modern knowledge economies, products are often decisions. Why do we not think about how we make decisions at scale? We need to spend the same amount of time on decision design as we do on traditional, physical product design. It is worthwhile to rethink the decision-making in your company.

There are two things to do. First, ensure that your organization allows individual agile decision-making. Second, ensure that your organization has agile systems that support superior decision-making. The following section will help you to carry this out.

IMPLEMENTING AGILE DECISION-MAKING

INDIVIDUAL DECISION-MAKING

There are many recipes and approaches to make decisions. In summary, individual decision-making follows five steps:

1. Define the context
2. Select the options
3. Know the consequences
4. Balance conflicting demand
5. Mitigate the risks

Use Tool #20, Make Your Choice, to think through your decisions.

JUDGEMENT

Good judgement is the dividing capability between executives and leaders. It is the foundation for superior, smart decisions that deliver the expected results.

With the right judgement in the specific situation and context, everything else is comparably unimportant. Top leaders are characterized by the number of good decisions they make.

In most cases, the consequences of the decisions of executives are huge. Their choices impact the lives of others. Executives in agile organizations make decisions every day. These are smaller and bigger decisions. But it is the judgement of executives that determines the success of an organization. As such, good judgement is the dividing capability in every organization.

The ability to gauge a situation is a key criterion of judgement. Single decision can lead to very different results. Executives need to spend time to understand the context within which they make decisions.

In organizations, the context is determined by managerial systems that offer measurement, direction, implementation, beliefs and boundary guidance. Systems exist as rules, routines and tools that help people to know with clarity, move in one direction, mobilize the energy, maintain the focus, be efficient, reload energy and use the space.

In the context of these systems, executives check whether their decisions are aligned with the overall guidance of the organization. As such, systems create the context for good decision-making. This context gains importance in a knowledge-driven environment where executives make decisions every day.

DYNAMIC SYSTEMS FOR PEOPLE-CENTRIC MANAGEMENT

Figure 40 lists the requirements of individual decision-making systems for decision-making at scale in organizations. The design of systems with dynamic features is the prerequisite to establish leadership everywhere.

Levers	Individual requirements	Organizational requirements
Know with clarity	Awareness, purpose	Raise awareness, help people to find purpose and self-responsibility, introduce routines that reduce complexity
Move in one direction	Choice, relationships	Enable choice, connect people to enhance knowledge, delegate, ensure that rules can handle ambiguity
Mobilize the energy	Trust, collaboration	Build trust to reduce uncertainty; facilitate collaboration, self-organization and leadership interactions
Maintain the focus	Focus of attention, learning	Focus attention, enable learning, implement broad direction, introduce tools to deal with volatility
Be efficient	Time	Momentum, routine, cycle
Reload energy	Investment in attention and time	Direct attention, implement flow strategies, encourage healthy stress, engaging culture
Use your space	Accountability	Workplace, structures
Decision-making	Understand context, make the decision and act on it	Management systems to understand, think, act, behave

FIGURE 40: AGILE DECISION-MAKING

Individuals search for flow. Organizations demand performance. The bridge comes from designing decision-making with dynamic features.

ROUTINES

Key routines: feedback, strategy development, budgeting, management by objectives, risk management

Routines help us to be efficient and effective by following procedures for repetitive tasks. To cope with growing complexity, routines need to create awareness rather than control. Complexity is like water; it cannot be compacted. Better awareness is the only way to deal with increased complexity.

Traditional ways of addressing complexity include deconstructing it, setting goals and delegating decision-making. Increased complexity is frequently a cause of ineffective, bureaucratic routines and managerial processes. The fix for this is a dynamic design that establishes a balance between judgement and rigour. Prevent an emphasis on control by designing routines that enable higher levels of awareness and help people find purpose.

RULES

Key rules: measurement, strategy and performance management, governance.

Rules set the boundaries for decisions and actions. In times of increasing ambiguity, rules must enable choice. When the future is unclear, choice in decision-making performs better than standard operating procedures. Greater ambiguity is frequently a cause of 'infected' rules and the lack of discipline to follow them. Agility and speed in dealing with ambiguities require a dynamic design for choice and relationships.

INTERACTIONS

Key interactions: sense-making, strategy conversation, contribution dialogues and risk dialogues.

As most work requires more than one person, interactions are the means to align and cooperate on work. To cope with rising levels of uncertainty, leaders need to trust rather than command. The only way to deal with uncertainty is to trust in your own abilities. With increasing uncertainty, it is important to define a management policy that balances responsibility and outside control. The fix for flawed leadership is to better design interactions to improve relationships and support collaboration. To prevent creeping uncertainty from hampering performance, interactions require a dynamic design with features that enable trust and collaboration.

TOOLS

Key tools: performance metrics, strategy, plans, goals, vision, mission, values.

Tools support work and leadership. To address greater volatility, tools must focus attention rather than aim. When things change quickly, people need something they can hold on to. Use tools that focus attention on what is important. Amid increasing volatility and market dynamics, it is important to get the control policy right, such that it offers a balance between enabling self-initiative and fostering goal achievement. The way to fix erroneous tools is to ensure that they are appropriately designed for purpose and collaboration. Prevent focus on the wrong things by using dynamic tools that help people to focus their attention and learn, rather than just enabling control.

CYCLE

Key cycle: corporate.

In an agile context, high individual efficiency and the productive use of time come from following an agile cycle. Agile organizations maintain a corporate cycle that guides the 'big' management processes, such as strategy, reviews, performance management and risk management. A dynamically designed corporate cycle facilitates decision-making throughout the organization.

CULTURE

Key feature: organizational energy.

Culture is the result of productive organizational energy. And energy is the result of invested attention and time. As such, executive leadership and managerial systems determine much of the culture in organizations. The challenge of maintaining a productive culture is to limit the interference of viruses that willingly or unwillingly creep into managerial systems every now and then to unstick the corporate glue.

WORKPLACE

Key features: accountability structure, workplace.

Accountability defines executive space. Structures emerges from accountabilities that balance spans of control, accountability, influence and support. Digital communications technologies have fundamentally altered the workplace. For many tasks, physical presence is no longer necessary. Agile workplaces are flexible and independent of location, and they facilitate connectivity and collaboration. Places to meet become the means to build relationships and grow knowledge.

SYSTEMS

Managerial systems guide individual decision-making in organizations with rules, routines and tools. Dynamic systems have a design that caters to people. They support executives to make decisions.

It is now time for your Decision Break. You can also use Tool #20, Make Your Choice, to explore your decision-making.

MY DECISION BREAK

 What challenges do you face in making decisions?

 How do you make decisions?

 How can you ensure good decision-making at scale in your organization?

Nudge #12 was about decisions, decision-making, judgement and systems. These give agile management with distributed leadership the competitive advantage in the 21st-century knowledge era. The next nudge is about introducing leadership everywhere – making the inner game, the use of resources, accountability and decision-making work for everyone in the organization.

DECISIONS

In the knowledge era, all people are executives. They apply the principles of the inner game and use their resources the agile way. As such, they assume leadership roles and make better decisions.

KEY SECTION IDEAS

- Agile decision-making relies on the inner game and individual resources
- Judgement is the dividing skill for leaders
- Decision-making at scale requires systems with a design oriented around people

ACTION AGENDA

- Review how you make decisions – use Tool #20, Make Your Choice
- Use the Decision Break to think about decision-making at scale in your organization
- Use Tool #20, Make Your Choice, to make your choice for agile

FURTHER READING

On judgment: Tichy, M. N. and Bennis, W. E. (2007). Making judgement calls: The ultimate act of leadership. *Harvard Business Review*, October. Accessed 23 April 2020. https://hbr. org/2007/10/making-judgment-calls.

CHAPTER 6

Leadership Everywhere

With the inner game, agile resources and agile decision-making, you now have the opportunity to establish leadership everywhere and unlock the talent of your employees to face the challenges of a dynamic era. Nudge #13 is about how we establish leadership everywhere, starting with people-centricity and developing agile as an organizational and managerial capability at scale.

Agile work unlocks the skills of talents and removes organization interference. By tapping into their resources, organizations can deal with dynamic environments. In the knowledge era, executives make decisions. Agile offers the opportunity to distribute accountability and establish leadership everywhere. The benefits are multiple: your organization will get the mileage it deserves from the talent that it engages; the talent will balance traditional and agile better than any system can do; and agile will help you to focus on clients and to drive innovation, growth and performance in ways that create value for society.

NUDGE #13: UNLOCK THE TALENT

Your people-centric mind-shift will unlock the *talent* and distribute leadership everywhere.

People-centricity unlocks the talents of your people via the following:

- **Self-responsibility**: Leaders use motivation based on purpose
- **Delegation**: Leaders trust in Self 2 and apply their knowledge and skills
- **Self-organization**: Leaders invest time and attention and release productive energy to bring out the greatness of others
- **Attention**: Leaders use a wide focus of attention to tap into their talents' energy, learn and be creative

THE PEOPLE-CENTRIC SHIFT

The shift to people-centricity first and foremost requires a mind-shift: from heroic leadership to leadership everywhere with collective minds and from traditional to agile organizations and management

(Figure 41). The shift fundamentally alters our work environment and how we perform and use resources, and requires a toolbox that is designed around people making decisions.

In a people-centric organization, the work environment shifts from delivering tangible outcomes to applying knowledge to create intangible products. People apply the inner game to cope with the challenges of the outer game and therefore act on their own. They rely on their own resources to get work done. The focus shifts from power to unlocking talents. And the dynamic toolbox supports delegated decision-making.

	From traditional...	...to people-centricity
Work environment (outer game)	Stable, transactions, tangible	Dynamic, knowledge, intangible
Performance (inner game)	Plan-do-check-act	Awareness, choice, trust
Resources	Power	Energy, focus of attention, time, space, accountability
Toolbox	Hierarchy, separation of thinking and doing	Dynamic tools and decision-making

FIGURE 41: THE PEOPLE-CENTRIC SHIFT

For most executives, the shift to people-centricity and the choice of agile are not part of their experience. They have been domesticated in a context that has always required traditional and tangible forms of control, power and hierarchy.

THE AGILE TIPPING POINT

The shift to people-centricity does not come for free. For most of us, traditional ways of doing things are known and deeply anchored in our habits. Overcoming our habits and leaving behind things that have worked in the past requires energy. However, from many successful transformations, my organization has observed that the investment in attention and time reaches a tipping point (Figure 42) where the energy becomes productive and the results become visible.

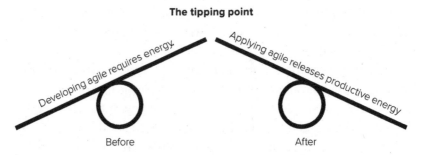

The tipping point

Developing agile requires energy

Applying agile releases productive energy

Before

After

FIGURE 42: THE AGILE TIPPING POINT

The tipping point is one of those defining moments when flow occurs and the return to traditional is no longer an option. Leaders who have 'crossed the Rubicon' to agile explain that energy flows, that they have recovered time for important things and that their focus of attention enables them to continuously learn and adapt.

A TRANSFORMATION

In the 21st century, the idea of transformation has become popular. However, the word is overused, often empty and little understood. We should not use 'transformation' lightly. A transformation is not just another change. It is a change of energy in form, appearance and structure that fundamentally alters decision-making, behaviours and actions. Transformation means creating something new that has not existed before, and that cannot be determined in advance. Transformation is learning and applied new knowledge, and requires experience.

The first step is transformation of the individual. It comes about through awareness, insights and learning about the system that determines how we and organizations function and operate. Self-responsibility, motivation and initiative are necessary to stretch beyond the normal. The inner game offers the structure required for the necessary mental process and paradigm shift in learning and performance.

The transformation of an organization requires the courage to lead a journey into the unknown. While agile offers essential principles, their application is new for most people and organizations. We can expect different outcomes in different organizations. The transformation itself involves the continuous creation of awareness, insights and learning opportunities on the theory of agile management – a theory that is highly individual and, therefore, will become your own way of doing things. There is no general theory to apply. Your organization's theory will become your management model.

Beliefs, patterns, habits and paradigms dominate management theories and how they are implemented. Our assumptions determine how we structure accountability, how we interact, and the rules, routines and tools of our systems (Figure 43). As a result, different organizations' structures, leadership processes and systems result in different decisions, actions and behaviours. Transformation challenges our assumptions.

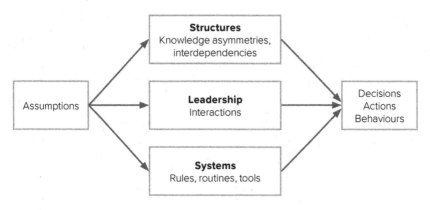

FIGURE 43: A TRANSFORMATION

DIAGNOSTIC MENTORING

Diagnostic mentoring (Figure 44) guides the transformation from data to action in line with Argyris' Ladder of Inference (Argyris, 1990; Senge, 1990). Diagnostics establish the observation points on operations. The Performance Triangle (see Figure 13) connects the elements in a model that creates meaning. People-centric levers (see Section #3 of Chapter 2) facilitate the questioning of assumptions. Four operating modes (see Chapter 1) offer choice on what management model best fits the business model. Awareness and insights (see Chapter 3) create inferences that can inform your choice of and shift to people-centricity. Learning is reflection. It creates new knowledge, and new knowledge leads to new experiences.

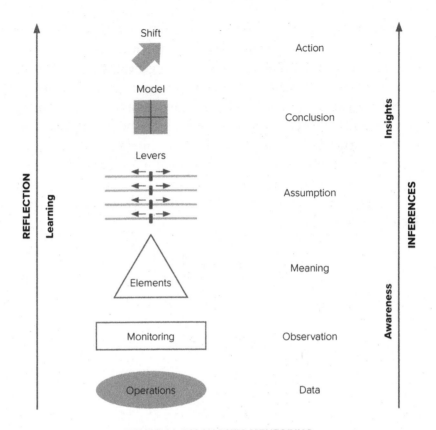

FIGURE 44: DIAGNOSTIC MENTORING

Use Tool #21, Start with Your Team, to involve your team in your choice of agile.

POSITIVE ASSUMPTIONS

Agile settings start by making various positive assumptions about people:

- Self-responsible people become more knowledgeable
- Knowledge among employees migrates decisions downwards (Figure 45)
- Employees are executives – they make decisions at the client front guided by broad direction and a wide focus of attention
- Self-organization requires managers and employees to spend more time interacting, sharing, aligning and coordinating

- Leaders must use interactive leadership in decentralized structures with dynamic systems

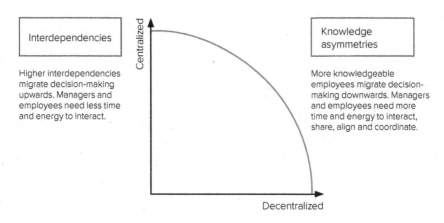

FIGURE 45: INTERDEPENDENCIES AND KNOWLEDGE

These assumptions are fundamentally different from those of traditional settings, which tend to make negative assumptions about people:

- People need control and managers have all the knowledge
- Higher interdependencies migrate decisions-making upwards (Figure 45)
- Managers with power make decisions – they use bureaucratic systems that reserve time and energy for control
- The role of the leader is to command in centralized structures with traditional control systems

Agile structures remove dependencies and assume that people have knowledge and talent. This requires scaling systems that balance agility with stability and individualizing leadership (Figure 46) that enables control through interaction. Scaling adds agile where people need to deal with increasing volatility, uncertainty, complexity and ambiguity. Talented people are different from each other. They come with different ambitions, talents and skills. Individualizing leadership adds agile in ways that help every individual to unlock their talent and contribute to create value.

SCALING AND INDIVIDUALIZING

Individualizing and scaling require ambidextrous capabilities from employees, leaders and the operating system. Stress, conflicts and role ambiguity limit individuals' ability to be ambidextrous. Diversity in leadership teams is a key factor in following an ambidextrous strategy. Leaders with diverse backgrounds and teams with different experiences are more likely to explore new directions and capabilities while maintaining their current operations. In contrast, integrating individualizing and scaling functions so that they are the responsibility of one person tends not to work and reduces overall ambidexterity. What works is for leaders to use individualizing leadership and for top management to ensure that managerial systems are designed to be scaled.

FIGURE 46: SCALING AND INDIVIDUALIZING

Agile demands interactions with individuals. Interactions are an effective means of control. Agile interactions are individual – specific to every person. The shift to people-centricity requires leaders to be out at the client front, interacting with stakeholders and interfering as the means to exercise control. As interactions will become more intense and take up larger parts of senior executives' time, it makes sense to delegate some of the organizing and planning work to a chief of staff (in case of a CEO), an assistant (in case of senior leaders) or junior managers (for other leaders). They can bring you time to be with your people at the client front. Chiefs of staff can triage data and feed to leaders what they need to lead.

Scaling and individualizing are two complementary features required to make the choice of agile. Scaling enables systems to operate in a dynamic environment, and individualizing updates leadership in the context of distributed knowledge. Interventions in any operating system are transformations, as they alter the behaviours, decisions and actions of people in organizations.

Agile transformations are motivated either by the need to change (e.g. to bring about a significant breakthrough so as to pursue new opportunities) or by a leader who is driven by the urgency of a vision to create the future. From either motivation, the entire mindset and paradigm are forced to shift with an unknown outcome. Along that journey, structures, leadership and systems emerge and are created through continuous learning and actions never taken before.

Agile transformations alter structures, leadership and systems. The transformation method requires awareness, insights and learning. Awareness comes through capability and resource monitoring with diagnostics that continuously review, test, question and challenge the implementation of management theory. With these insights, a journey of learning starts that establishes new management models that were not known before.

A TEAM EFFORT

The decision to undertake a transformation with an unknown outcome comes with fear. It takes courage and clear intent: awareness, to know with clarity. But leadership would be a safe place if all answers were already known. Transformation is a team effort and the choice to move in one direction. Practice has shown that any successful transformation requires architects, translators and doers (Figure 47) who trust their talents and are able to mobilize their energy.

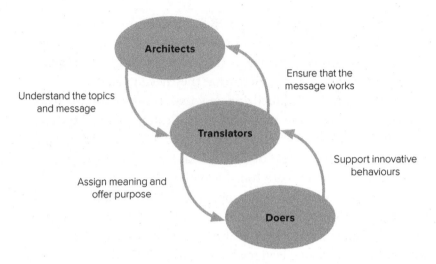

FIGURE 47: A TEAM EFFORT

Architects are the experts on the design of management, organizations and transformations. They can help you to create the agile systems that will best work for your organization. Translators are experts in communications. They can turn your agile message into interactions as events, training and experiences that support the transformation effort. Doers are executives with accountability for parts of the organization, and they lead the transformation in their units. Their task is to maintain the focus that stimulates further learning.

It is my hypothesis that most managers don't have a theory of management with a distinct management model they intend to create. All managers use some form of management. In the absence of a theory, there is central command-and-control based on luck. Because management in practice and theory is invisible but deeply rooted in any organization's culture, there is the accepted attitude that we should 'not wake up a sleeping dog' – just get on with things. The agile transformation is a paradigm shift in line with the four people-centric levers (self-organization, delegation, self-responsibility and focus of attention) that ensures clarity on the intended management theory, follows a deliberate management model, and includes emergent practices through knowledge about what works best. New knowledge is obtained through learning.

THE AGILE DESTINATION
OF SEVEN EXECUTIVES

Having introduced the inner game, resources and decision-making, let us now look at the conclusions of the seven executives' agile journeys. Awareness and insights facilitated their ongoing learning about agile.

The chief executive of the large insurance company raised awareness of agile with the insights from the online Agile Diagnostic. Additionally, using the Performance Triangle (see Figure 13), he established a shared language for a successful transformation to agile. With this foundation, he initiated learning by engaging 250 key leaders worldwide in training on people-centric levers and their effects on entrepreneurial behaviours that can establish a performance culture. Simultaneously, his staff replaced bureaucratic systems with routines and tools designed to support the talent. Just one year after the programme was initiated, the control diagnostic (a repeat of the Agile Diagnostic) reported 25% higher scores on just about all leadership dimensions.

The manager of the global pharmaceutical company created awareness with 80 managers in the US, Europe and Asia to distil the key issues. By engaging all his leaders in developing a carefully crafted development roadmap, he initiated the learning that would turn traditional into agile. Simultaneously, he changed the agenda of his executive team meeting to include metrics that would capture the effects of the roadmap on innovation and results. After one year, the control diagnostic showed higher scores on most agile elements and a 50% increase in the innovation score. The development work continued.

The architect and chief of staff of a global think-tank raised awareness of agile via a diagnostic poster session that created insights into the concept of agile architecture among management and the organization. Next, he initiated changes in managerial systems and the annual cycle that would make his operation more flexible, and at the same time establish an agenda for the talent to work on between events. Within a couple of years, the core staff had grown from 200 to over 500 people with a management model that fit the needs of the business.

The translator and CEO office manager of a South African food producer created awareness with the Agile Diagnostic that revealed the need to redesign the organization's managerial processes to better guide the work of the executive team. Through redesigning the CEO office and the key managerial processes with agile features, she was able to better translate the CEO's vision into an agenda and cycle that would support the hybrid context the company required, which would combine the rigour of traditional processes with agile. Over time, the executive team established a culture with 25% higher scores on agile, effectiveness and innovation.

The integrator and manager of the mid-sized city in the US established awareness in his leadership team with the Agile Diagnostic. He then engaged all leaders to use the same workshop template to develop agile work across 12 departments. In this way, he implemented his organization-wide agenda and found better ways to work and administrate the city. The result was a culture that increased employee engagement by 50% and with it agility and service responsibility.

The chair of the Middle Eastern sugar company achieved a high level of awareness with his management team through the continued use of the Agile Diagnostic. In this way, he ensured that the organization remained on track with its development. He installed managerial systems that scaled in line with growth and engaged his team to work with new members to 'work in the system' (see Chapter 1). Within a few years, the start-up grew into one of the world's largest sugar manufacturing plants.

The executive coach with clients who needed to make the shift to people-centricity continued to use the practices in this book and the Agile Diagnostic with visual design thinking to work with her clients to first make the shift as individuals and then to transform the organization.

Awareness and insights are the keys to initiating an agile transformation. They are the prerequisites for people and organizations to learn and successfully make the shift to people-centricity.

Nudge #13 introduced the agile transformation and the need for genuine leadership to get there. The shift to people-centricity requires experience. But people-centricity is an experience that most leaders don't have. The good news is that talents apply their learning and use motivation to lead the way. This book offers the outside knowledge that several authors note is essential for any transformation (Deming, 1993; Joiner, 1994; Senge, 1999).

With this, now is your time to demonstrate leadership. Take the Shift Break and initiate your last nudge towards transformation. Experimental learning is how initiate the transformation within your organization.

MY SHIFT BREAK

 What challenges do you face in your shift to people-centricity and agile? Use Tool #21, Start with Your Team.

 How can you make this shift happen?

 How can you ensure that agile becomes your organization's choice?

LEADERSHIP EVERYWHERE

The choice of agile involves a transformation to embrace self-responsibility, delegation, self-organization and purpose.

KEY CHAPTER IDEAS

- Agile requires a mind-shift that fundamentally alters work, performance, organization and management
- Agile is initiated via a shift to people-centricity
- For most executives, agile is not part of their experience
- Agile development must reach a tipping point before it shows its benefits
- The transformation involves scaling systems and individualizing leadership
- Architects, translators and doers can support you with the transformation

ACTION AGENDA

- Take the Shift Break to think about how to engage your team in agile
- Use Tool #21, Start with Your Team, to prepare for the engagement of your team

FURTHER READING

On the external perspective: Deming, W. E. (1993). *The New Economics*. Cambridge: MIT Press.

On the transformation: Michel, L. (2020). *People-Centric Management: How Managers Use Four Levers to Bring Out the Greatness of Others*. London: LID Business Media.

On the agile design: Michel, L. (2017). *Management Design: Managing People and Organizations in Turbulent times* (2nd ed.). London: LID Publishing.

CHAPTER 7

Experiential Learning

In the previous chapter, we explored why people-centricity and agile are different and, for most of us, not part of our experience. The choice of agile is a transformation that is initiated via a personal mind-shift. Nudge #14 expands on the inner game, the agile use of resources and decision-making as the experience that is needed to make the shift – personally, for your team and for your organization.

NUDGE #14: LEARN FROM NEW EXPERIENCES
Engage your team in agile.

THE INNER GAME, RESOURCES AND DECISIONS

Our mind is the product of the past, our experience. The mind is present when our nervous system, which resides in our brain and body, is activated. Mind is brain in action. It activates all our records of what we have learned and experienced in the past. These include habits, which are hardened and take a lot of energy to overcome.

Traditional minds assume that people need control to get things done – this is a negative assumption about people. As a consequence, they apply control, the dominant Anglo-Saxon management model. Agile minds rely on principles such as self-responsibility and delegation, which are based on positive assumptions about people.

Our thinking turns material thoughts into chemical information. When we activate thinking that we have activated before, patterns of the past are linked. The same thinking repeats, the same emotions continue. We call this 'conditioning.' Habits dominate as our auto-pilot, with the same thoughts, behaviours, actions and emotions. While this is very helpful for our daily life, it prevents us from digesting new things and learning. With the same routines, tomorrow is always the same. To change our condition, we need to change our thinking and feeling.

Traditional routines and habits have trained our minds the traditional way. That is our experience. The choice of agile requires a different experience – the experience of the benefits of agile, which most leaders don't have. The switch from traditional to agile experience happens through learning.

Learning connects neurons and updates the brain. New patterns are created when we pay attention to knowledge and information that makes sense to us and when we interact with the external world. Something new is 'printed' as a story in our brain that reinforces the connections. Learning creates these new connections. Now, we are at a new stage. And every time we remember something, we maintain our connections.

For most traditional leaders, new things, agile ways of doing things and delegating power to talented people feel like losing control. Overcoming that traditional state of mind and fear requires the individual to make the mind-shift to agile. The shift requires a state of mind and belief that agile and enabling people are superior to traditional control.

Changing energy requires clear intentions and strong emotions that create awareness so as to attract new experience. The good news is that to attract new experience, we just need to pay attention and be aware.

It takes leadership with a clear intent (mind) and strong emotion (heart) to change our biology from the past to the future. Mind and body together impact matter and we can create reality. Feedback helps us to understand whether we are doing things right. If we change the feelings and thoughts within us, we can see the change outside us. That's how we make agile a habit.

Agile by Choice is intended to raise your awareness, offer agile insights and provide learning opportunities to help you shift your mindset and embrace agile – and thereby unlock talent and develop leadership everywhere. The inner game (principles), the agile use of resources and superior decisions – how humans can best manage and use their talents – are the means to get there.

ENGAGING THE TEAM

Now, with your personal shift to people-centricity, you are ready to engage your team in the same way you have made your journey through experiential learning. Assume that your talents are *motivated* and want to *learn* to gain that experience fast. This learning involves an investment in the skills required to play the inner game, use resources the agile way and make better decisions. Architects, translators and doers will support you in the shift.

Experiential learning is the cycle that establishes leadership everywhere, develops agile, offers client focus and drives performance. It applies the inner game (awareness, choice, trust and focus) to build experience among your team. At the same time, it uses the inner game to lead the agile way. Understanding the principles of the inner game is easy. Applying them requires skill and dedication.

Experiential learning (Figure 48) simultaneously involves 'work *on* the system' and 'work *in* the system' (see Chapter 1). Start in one place in your organization and then expand the idea across all other units. Don't experiment – one does not experiment with people. Do it as a means to improve work, organization and management.

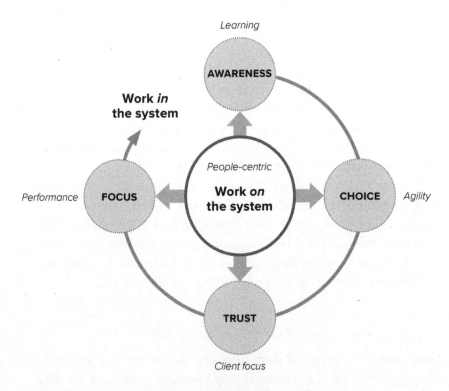

FIGURE 48: EXPERIENTIAL LEARNING

Leadership everywhere is the goal. Awareness initiates the learning to get you started. Agile is your choice of leadership style. It replaces traditional change, which never worked anyway. Trust your team to care about clients. Focus your attention for superior performance, innovation and growth.

Experience is the opposite of education. It combines 'work *on* the system' with 'work *in* the system.' Don't educate your leaders in yet another executive development programme. Engage them in creating systems that support the agile journey. Use *Agile by Choice* to guide your team and your organization with the following learning opportunities (which correspond with the nudges found throughout this book):

#1   **Map your challenges**: use your context to initiate agile

#2   **Explore the dimensions**: use individual and institutional dimensions of agile

#3   **Engage your inner game**: apply awareness, choice and trust to reach flow

#4   **Turn on your lights**: use awareness to reach clarity on agile

#5   **It's your choice**: rely on Self 2 to confirm agile

#6   **Trust yourself and your team**: mobilize all resources to make agile their way

#7   **Return on management**: invest in energy, attention and time

#8   **Power up your energy**: balance agile engagement and refuelling

#9   **Focus your attention**: learn to perform with agile

#10   **Maintain the momentum**: keep the pace on agile

#11   **Create your space**: use the agile accountability template

#12   **Establish leadership everywhere**: develop agile decision-making

#13   **Unlock the talent**: the agile mind-shift will make everyone a leader

#14   **Learn from new experiences**: engage everyone to work on agile

THE AGILE JOURNEY

Agile by Choice creates the learning experience you need to successfully master your choice of agile. Awareness, insights and learning guide your journey (Figure 49) with techniques, tools and frameworks to engage your team.

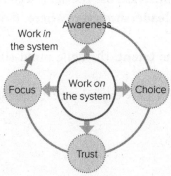

FIGURE 49: AWARENESS, INSIGHTS AND LEARNING

Create awareness of agile: The Agile Diagnostic (Tool #4) establishes observation points. Monitoring is a discipline that can be used to observe and alter design. By observing (scanning) capabilities, potential faults and malfunctions can be spotted at an early stage. By becoming aware of critical signals, potential design requirements can be identified. In this way, leaders can decide whether or not to address issues. As such, monitoring initiates design changes relating to capabilities.

Act on your insights on agile: The Performance Triangle (see Figure 13) distils the elements of agile. The use of agile capabilities and design is selective. The decision to employ a specific design excludes other alternatives. The design process is about the selection of managerial tools, routines and rules that make organizations agile. Design requires reflection and interactions. It is not free from politics. The setting of these conversations determines much about the design's quality.

Expedite the agile way of learning: The inner game offers the techniques to follow the agile way of learning. Monitoring assumes that the design is reversible and not frozen. While deeply embedded in organizational practices and rooted in the past, managerial design and capabilities can be changed through interventions. The people-centric shift guides specific capability development projects in line with decisions on what needs to be changed. In this way, the idea of permanent change is replaced by the idea of combining learning and doing. It is an iterative process.

MAKING AGILE WORK

With the same routines, tomorrow is always the same. Successful leaders change their condition, their thinking and their feeling. Only if you are in a powerful place beyond space and time where matter emerges (see Chapter 4) can you initiate real change. Figure 50 summarizes the steps and activities you and your executives can take to activate experiential learning with the tools and dimensions contained in this book. Use the work templates to get started. Your last nudge before it's your turn to implement agile is the Experiential Learning Break. Use Figure 50 to make your choice of agile work in your organization.

This is what *Agile by Choice* is all about: the executive experience, the essential agile decision and the practice of the inner game, which mobilize all of your resources to make the shift to people-centricity.

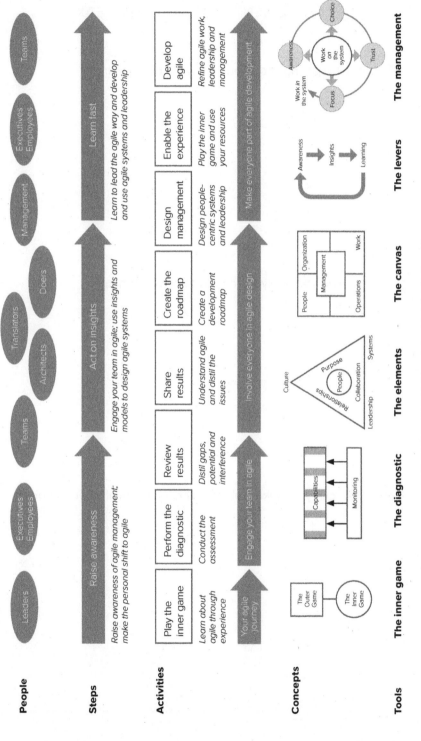

People

Leaders · Executives Employees · Teams · Translators · Architects · Doers · Management · Executives Employees · Teams

Steps

Raise awareness — Raise awareness of agile management; make the personal shift to agile

Act on insights — Engage your team in agile: use insights and models to design agile systems

Learn fast — Learn to lead the agile way and develop and use agile systems and leadership

Activities

Play the inner game	Perform the diagnostic	Review results	Share results	Create the roadmap	Design management	Enable the experience	Develop agile
Learn about agile through experience	Conduct the assessment	Distil gaps, potential and interference	Understand agile and distil the issues	Create a development roadmap	Design people-centric systems and leadership	Play the inner game and use your resources	Refine agile work, leadership and management

Your agile journey → Engage your team in agile → Involve everyone in agile design → Make everyone part of agile development

Concepts

The inner game · The diagnostic · The elements · The canvas · The levers · The management

Tools

The inner game: The Outer Game / The Inner Game

The diagnostic: Capabilities / Monitoring

The elements: Culture, Purpose, People, Collaboration, Systems, Leadership, Relationships

The canvas: People, Organization, Management, Operations, Work

The levers: Awareness → Insights → Learning

The management: Awareness, Choice, Trust, Focus, Work on the system, Work in the system

FIGURE 50: MAKE YOUR CHOICE OF AGILE WORK

MY EXPERIENTIAL LEARNING BREAK

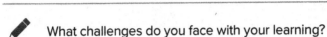 What challenges do you face with your learning?

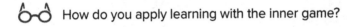 How do you apply learning with the inner game?

How can you make agile learning your organization's choice?

EXPERIENTIAL LEARNING

The successful shift from the idea of agile to action only comes through experience and practice. Experiential learning makes the shift happen.

KEY CHAPTER IDEAS

- Experience comes from investment in your own skills around playing the inner game, using resources the agile way and implementing better decision-making

ACTION AGENDA

- Use the 14 nudges to initiate the agile transformation in your organization
- Create awareness, offer insights and facilitate learning
- Use the Experiential Learning Break to initiate the people-centric shift

FURTHER READING

On people-centric: Michel, L. (2020). *People-Centric Management: How Leaders Use Four Levers to Bring Out the Greatness of Others.* London: LID Publishing.

Tools

Here are 21 tools to help you make the choice of agile.

#1   **The Virus Check**: scan through the symptoms of non-agile

#2   **My Challenge Map**: align potential and resources

#3   **Take a Break**: STOP and think

#4   **Agile Diagnostic**: identify agile maturity and potential

#5   **Review Stakeholders**: determine what they want and what you want

#6   **Document Agile**: consider assumptions, principles, potential, gaps and initiatives

#7   **Get into the Flow**: use these steps to reach flow more often

#8   **Create Awareness**: use these steps to reach higher awareness and attention

#9   **It's Your Choice**: practise to reach clarity

#10   **Examine Trust**: review the trust you have in your team

#11   **Review Commitment**: test the balance of give and take

#12   **Check Your Energy**: conduct a body, mind, emotions and spirit health check

#13   **Refuel Your Energy**: plan your next stop

#14   **Pay Attention**: review your span of attention

#15   **Time Accounts**: take account of how you spend time

#16   **101 on Executive Time**: follow the essentials of time management

#17   **Pace Your Time**: identify time consumers

#18   **Executive Pace**: learn about ways to find time

#19   **Accountability Profile**: define your space

#20   **Make Your Choice**: learn about how to make decisions

#21   **Start with Your Team**: create awareness, share insights and learn from others

#1:
THE VIRUS CHECK

Agile starts with you as a leader. If you recognize any of the following symptoms, then use Agile by Choice as your workbook and personal journey to identify the root causes of interference and fix the issues that keep you from getting to people-centric faster.

 Do any of the following viruses resonate with your organization?

PEOPLE:

Fault with people: Hands on the people, instead of the problem.
Busyness: We like to be busy. We are so efficient that we don't have time to think.
Status: We like to label people and value function, which leads us to evaluate their contribution by grade, not competence.

CULTURE:

Forwards to the past: We look for the future in reports about the past (results). We are so afraid of losing our heritage that we won't change our culture.
Crisis jumping: In a crisis, we act quickly and decisively, then we often wait for the next crisis to hit before similar actions occur.
Full sponge: We have a capacity problem with too many projects and changes. It is difficult to know what matters most and we are stressed out.

LEADERSHIP:

Command-and-control: We like management to tell us how to run the company, so we don't feel any personal accountability when things go wrong.

Flavour of the month: We jump from change to change in separate, not integrated, initiatives; cynicism about new 'change programmes' mounts.

Disjoint action: We don't see the big picture and how our unit's work relates to the group or fits in with the overall strategy.

SYSTEMS:

Engineering oriented, to a fault: We find the ideal technical solution at the expense of getting to a solution fast.

What more than why: We think more about what needs to happen than why and who.

Process mania: We are so consumed by processes that not much actually gets decided.

RELATIONSHIPS:

Turfism: My business vs. our business. We like to defend our turf, sometimes to the exclusion of what is in the company's best interests. For example, we like to hide behind our team, defending them against others.

Punish those who dare to question: Raising critical questions is sign of disloyalty and insubordination.

All things to all people: We are not clearly focused on a few critical priorities. Each good idea receives attention and energy.

PURPOSE:

Blind obedience: When told, we do, even to a fault and even if we think it's wrong.

Results rule: We like results any way, any time and anyhow. It is nice to achieve results that fit our principles, but we only do so when we have time or can 'afford' it.

Moving targets: Things keep changing as we go.

COLLABORATION:

Hero worship: We like heroes. We like to label projects, initiatives and branches according to specific individuals, not the collective.

Narcissistic competitiveness: We like to win as individuals.

Authority ambiguity: In our complex matrix structure, we are not sure who has ultimate accountability and authority, so no one really does.

Extend this list by adding your favourites if you wish.

#2:
MY CHALLENGE MAP

Agile is about your business. Identify your business challenges with the following steps. They will offer your opportunities for people-centric management.

 Challenges

First, identify your challenges. What are your most important business challenges? Make a list.

A. _____

B. _____

C. _____

D. _____

E. _____

F. _____

G. _____

👓 Insights

Second, transfer your challenges into the following map. Evaluate every challenge from 0 (not relevant) to 10 (highly relevant) on the four dimensions:

- **Expertise**: Your application (practice) and insights (theory). Can you apply your knowledge and experience?
- **Origination**: Your new thinking and readiness for new ways of getting things done. Does it require a new approach?
- **Time and attention**: Your investment in time and attention. Can you spend time and focus your attention?
- **Energy**: Your engagement of energy. Does it release productive energy?

Third, connect the dots for every dimension to get to a spider-line graph.

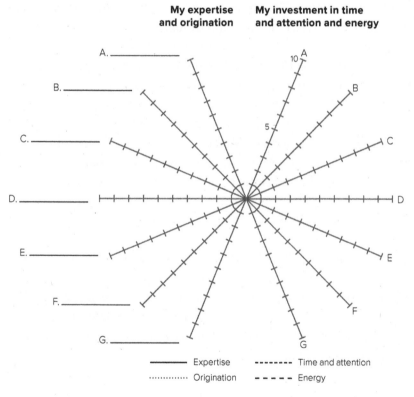

My expertise and origination   **My investment in time and attention and energy**

——— Expertise   - - - - - - - - Time and attention
·············· Origination   – – – – Energy

⊕ Decisions

Fourth, summarize your conclusions: Are you investing where it adds the most value? Are there ways you could be more effective? List your decisions.

#3:
TAKE A BREAK

Agile is the capacity to deal with a turbulent environment. In times of stress and higher challenges, it is time to take a break and reflect on your situation. Here are your people-centric steps to do that:

Relax: Put some distance between yourself and the current situation: your activities, emotions and thoughts.

Take time: Find the physical and mental environment that best supports your reflection and thinking. With your challenge in mind, answer the following questions: What do I want to achieve? What is the purpose? What is my agenda? Where does it come from? What are the priorities? Where is change needed? What direction should I be going in? The definition? What is the current momentum? What are the consequences? What are the critical performance variables? What is missing? What is the right question to ask? What do I want? Is it fun? Will it offer enjoyment? What does it mean for others? What are my assumptions? What resources can I mobilize? What is my mindset?

Get organized: Thinking does not organize itself. It helps to follow a distinct plan, model or strategy.

Move on: Thinking does not replace doing. Every stop requires a go. Take time for a break at the beginning and end of every day, every project and every change. Remove interference. Correct faulty communications. Learn.

#4:
AGILE DIAGNOSTIC

The choice of agile is a transformation. It fundamentally alters behaviours, decision-making, and the actions of leaders and employees. Success is not guaranteed. To raise your odds, this book has outlined the three steps – awareness, insights and learning – that you can follow to successfully make the shift to people-centricity. This diagnostic initiates the process.

The Agile Diagnostic offers 20 questions to help you establish a base from which to start, to debate priorities, and to decide on the choices for your transformation. The diagnostic is a structured way to gather input and knowledge so as to take a hard look at your organization. Clarity on the starting point dramatically increases success rates.

The Agile Diagnostic answers two questions:
1. How agile is your organization?
2. What can you do to develop people-centricity and agile?

Here is how to get started: answer Parts 1 and 2 of the questions by circling your scores.

With your answers to the questions in Parts 1 and 2, transfer your scores into the following visuals as you continue reading:

Operating Mode: Chapter 1, My Business Challenge Break. Answers 17-20.

People: Section #1 of Chapter 2, My People Dimension Break. Answers 12-15.

Organization: Section #2 of Chapter 2, My Organization Dimension Break: Answers 2-6.

Management: Section #3 of Chapter 2, My Management Dimension Break: Answers 17-20.

Work: Section #4 of Chapter 2, My Work Dimension Break: Answers 7-9.

Purpose: Section #4 of Chapter 2, My Purpose Break: Answers 2 and 4-6.

Relationships: Section #4 of Chapter 2, My Relationship Break: Answers 2 and 3.

Collaboration: Section #4 of Chapter 2, My Collaboration Break: Answers 3-6.

Operations: Section #5 of Chapter 2, My Operations Dimension Break: Answers 1-16.

Agile Maturity: Section #5 of Chapter 2, My Agile Maturity Break: Answers 1-16 (Calculate the Dynamic Capabilities score as per instructions on My Operations Dimension Break).

Then, for the people, organization and work dimensions, use coloured highlighters to mark every score as follows:

- **Green**: high scores, 80–100 = high agile capabilities
- **Yellow**: medium scores, 60–79 = medium agile capabilities
- **Red**: low scores, 0–59 = low agile capabilities

With the colours, your score become meaning.

QUESTIONS PART 1:
AGILE CAPABILITIES

	Strongly disagree	Disagree	Neutral	Agree	Strongly agree

Thinking about your organization's operating environment, answer the questions below:

1 We deliver on what we promise to our clients with an attractive strategy and the right capabilities.   0   13   25   37   50   63   75   88   100

2 Leaders and employees share the same understanding about how work is performed.   0   13   25   37   50   63   75   88   100

3 Leaders conduct productive conversations with employees regarding expectations and performance.   0   13   25   37   50   63   75   88   100

Thinking about your department's performance, answer the questions below:

4 Our management policies (e.g. decision-making rights, governance, performance and risk management) guide our decisions, actions and behaviours.   0   13   25   37   50   63   75   88   100

5 Our management processes (e.g. performance measurements and feedback, objectives agreements, business reviews) help us work effectively and efficiently.   0   13   25   37   50   63   75   88   100

6 Our management tools (e.g. performance indicators and targets, visions, values, strategies, risk limits, performance targets) help us set the right priorities and focus work on what matters most.   0   13   25   37   50   63   75   88   100

Thinking about your team dynamic, answer the questions below:

7 We can freely collaborate and exchange information across organizational boundaries for synergies and leverage.   0   13   25   37   50   63   75   88   100

8 We can rely on relevant relationships to support our work.   0   13   25   37   50   63   75   88   100

9 We are able to find purpose in what we do, establish a clear identity, and fully commit to our work.   0   13   25   37   50   63   75   88   100

In relation to how your organization competes and evolves, answer the questions below:

10 Our organization is renowned for innovation. We turn ideas into reality and add value to our clients' projects.   0   13   25   37   50   63   75   88   100

11 Our organization captures relevant opportunities and grows steadily.   0   13   25   37   50   63   75   88   100

Thinking about your own work ethic, answer the following questions:

12 I have access to relevant information and ask for feedback to gain clarity on important things.   0   13   25   37   50   63   75   88   100

13 I am able to focus and maintain my attention on important things without interferences.   0   13   25   37   50   63   75   88   100

14 I have the trust of my team and can mobilize the resources to get things done.   0   13   25   37   50   63   75   88   100

15 I have sufficient choice on what I need to do and how I perform those tasks.   0   13   25   37   50   63   75   88   100

16 At work, I can unfold my full potential, for example, freely use and apply all my knowledge, capabilities, and creativity.   0   13   25   37   50   63   75   88   100

QUESTIONS PART 2:
PEOPLE-CENTRIC POTENTIAL

	Strongly disagree	Disagree	Neutral	Agree	Strongly agree

Thinking about how your organization helps people to know with clarity, use the scale to answer these questions: Which statement best fits your situation?

17 Leaders keep information to themselves, tell people what to do, and check on their work   0 13 25 37 50 63 75 88 100   Self-responsible employees find purpose in what they are doing and get work done

Thinking about how your company moves in one direction, use the scale below to answer these questions: Which statement best fits your situation?

18 Leaders have the power and insights to make decisions. They determine work, set goals, and communicate direction   0 13 25 37 50 63 75 88 100   Knowledge is widely distributed with employees that make decisions on the client front and act on them

Thinking about how your organization mobilizes energy, use the scale below to answer these questions: Which statement best fits your situation?

19 Leaders engage in comprehensive budgeting and allocate resources   0 13 25 37 50 63 75 88 100   Self-organization is principles by which we allocate resources on demand and collaborate

Thinking about how your organizations maintains the focus, use the scale below to answer these questions: Which statement best fits your situation?

20 Leaders use a comprehensive set of metrics and detailed performance targets to implement strategy   0 13 25 37 50 63 75 88 100   Our leaders mentor employees on how to best focus attention with a broad set of directional goals

#5:
REVIEW
STAKEHOLDERS

Agile does not work in isolation. It caters to your stakeholders. What do your stakeholders want? What do they contribute? What do you want from them? The list below includes some generic stakeholders but feel free to substitute your own.

Stakeholder	What they want	What you want from them
Employees		
Customers		
Investors		
Suppliers		
Supervision		
Communities		

Then consider the following questions:
- What are the three most important stakeholder needs?
- What are the three most important needs that you have?
- Do they match?

Look for the balance in stakeholder needs and what you and your organization want. The balance comes from people-centric management.

#6:
DOCUMENT
AGILE

The canvas[6] below is your notes template while you work through Chapter 2, Five Leadership Dimensions, and document your thoughts about the agile features of your organization and the people-centric requirements of management.

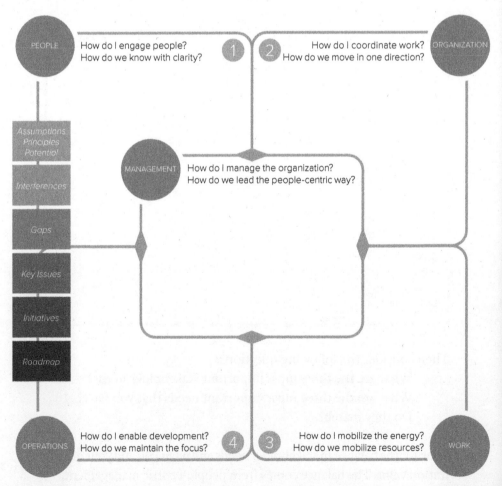

#7:
GET INTO
THE FLOW

Flow is the state where clarity, intent, head and heart merge. It's the state where people-centric features deliver agile outcomes.

Here are a few things you can do to get into the flow more often.

Be aware of your priorities and intent: Without passion for performance, the ambition to learn and the desire for enjoyment, you will lose your focus of attention more often and it will be harder to get it back and reach the flow zone. Therefore, clarify your intent and your priorities. Clarity will mobilize energies, strengthen your focus, pool your attention and bring you back into the flow zone.

Ensure feedback: Feedback should be immediate and direct. Short cycles allow for more intense flow experiences. More feedback means more power and control:

- Activate all your senses – be aware of yourself
- When receiving external information, don't get distracted, keep negative feedback within limits

Focus on the present:

- Have undivided attention: flow requires you to be in the present
- Be aware of the past but focus on your current tasks and on the now

Control the controllable:
- Search for the controllable elements in your work
- Control is the sense of safety and power, which is what people need, whereas a lack of control leads to self-trust and fear, which limit engagement
- Flow needs new challenges: a balance between challenges and control; to experience that, you need to stretch your limits

Have fun:
- Focus on having fun – your intrinsic motivation

#8:
CREATE
AWARENESS

Agile depends on awareness. Awareness is what you see when the light of focused attention shines. Here are five people-centric steps that you can use to raise your awareness of the challenge at hand.

BE AWARE

The better you can focus your attention, the faster you will be aware.
- **Triggers**: let your thoughts flow, and be open to finding associations through questions and visualizing your challenges.
- **Time**: Ideas and insights come fast. It may feel like time has stopped. How much time do you need to question and visualize?
- **Interference**: Rational thoughts often crowd our creativity and intuition. Keep that in mind.

Being aware requires physical, emotional and mental alignment. Here is your awareness test: to reach a high level of awareness, you need high scores. Circle the numbers that feel most appropriate to you and then write your total below.

Physical scale											
Tense	1	2	3	4	5	6	7	8	9	10	Relaxed
Emotional scale											
Negative	1	2	3	4	5	6	7	8	9	10	Positive
Mental scale											
Interfering	1	2	3	4	5	6	7	8	9	10	Focused

Reaching high awareness depends on finding balance in how you operate:

- **Make yourself comfortable**: Prevent any interference, be comfortable, remove tensions, be fully relaxed. Breathe.
- **Quiet your mind**: Choose a word, a sentence or a sound. Breathe and speak it out quietly over a couple of minutes. Count up to ten and down until you have reached full concentration.
- **Visualize**: Imagine an object that inspires you. Concentrate on it until your brain is empty.
- **Charge up**: Activate a symbol by finding an image or object that symbolizes power and energy to you. Activate your intrinsic motivation and use it to turn negative into positive.
- **Programme a trigger**: When you have reached high awareness, attach a symbol or sign to it such that you can trigger clarity by activating your trigger. Practice the trigger so that you can use it in challenging situations.

FOCUS ATTENTION

Concentrating to reaching high focus of attention is comparably easy. Focus is easily lost. Getting it back and maintaining it is more difficult.

For executives, dealing with challenges, difficult topics and questions is normally important, serious and emotional. This requires that you often need to focus your attention to reach a high degree of awareness and clarity. As such, it is important to be able to quickly activate the process and maintain it at a high level. Focus of attention requires energy, discipline and control.

Here is what you can do:

- Don't worry about how well you do this; view it as a game – the inner game
- Don't search for answers – they will come
- Be open to new insights
- Be aware – observe
- Keep focusing on the thing you need to think about
- Refocus. When sources of interference pop up, refocus your attention to regain your high level of awareness

IT'S YOUR CHOICE

Leaders have a tendency to start by clarifying their activities. But awareness starts with the intent.

The clearer the definition of the challenge, the clearer the intent. The clearer the intent, the more options are available. The better the options are, the more likely the solution to succeed.

Here is what you can do:

- Start with the question
- Ask yourself why it matters
- Focus on a metric that defines the intent
- Define the best approach

TRUST YOUR PERSPECTIVE

To raise the awareness on challenging situations and decisions, it is important to consider different perspectives. This may change your perspective but trust it once you have made the choice.

Changing perspective means:

- Seeing with other eyes
- Changing the time frame
- Seeing the bigger picture

VISUALIZE YOUR INTENT

Visualizing is the ability to use your imagination to see how to get to your intent. It is an ability that is not a given with most leaders.

Ensure that there is data and analysis to support your intuition.

Here is what you can do:

- Compare advantages and disadvantages
- Remove alternatives
- Compare options with a point of reference
- Calculate probabilities
- Evaluate trade-offs

#9:
IT'S YOUR CHOICE

Agile requires choice. And choice is the prerequisite for self-responsibility. It is the freedom you need to be able to make a choice. Here are some people-centric actions you can take when it's time to commit to agile as a critical choice.

FOCUS OF ATTENTION

Focus of attention is the means to reach high awareness. Focus of attention, especially in critical moments, is a distinctive skill of leaders. It is a discipline and performance that is invisible: the ability to focus all physical, mental and emotional resources on one thing.

YOUR CHOICE

After the fact, it is easy to judge any decision. It's an art to do it before you have made your choice. But you know when you've reached high awareness and made your choice. You will have experienced some of the following:
- Positive energy: good experience, enjoyment and energy
- Commitment to the solution: a feeling of being aligned with the intent
- Minimum interference after the moment

There is no leadership without this kind of awareness. The following criteria can be used as a test to determine whether a decision you are considering will be the right one:
- Saves time
- Reduces unnecessary activities
- Releases productive energies

- Projects the organization's purpose
- Focuses the team in one direction

THE FLOW STATE

The flow state is when utmost awareness leads to the obvious choice. This is what it feels like:

- **Emotions**: positive, satisfied, no fear, no worries, no doubts, full of energy, self-trust
- **Mental**: open, quiet, focused, controlled, in the now, aware
- **Physical**: quiet, relaxed

INTERFERENCE

Focus on Self 2 is how you deal with interference. Five common sources of interference are lack of direction, missing boundaries, emotions being out of control, lack of perspective and difficult options.

External interference can be removed or limited:

- **Multitasking**: avoid it as it stops you focusing
- **Competition**: compete with yourself; competition with others creates stress that you don't need
- **Take breaks**: Focus and awareness require energy; it takes time to refuel energy

#10:
EXAMINE
TRUST

Agile builds on trust. And trust is the fastest management concept. When there is trust, you can delegate decisions to people at the client front and short-cut lengthy approval processes throughout the ranks of hierarchy. To increase speed in your organization, you need to examine trust. This is why trust creates more value than any other management concept. Delegation depends on people-centric managers who trust their employees to get the job done.

 Here is your trust test: list the members of your team. Then rate every member with respect to the trust you have in them.

My team   Levels of trust: ++   + +/− − −−

1. _____

2 _____

3 _____

4 _____

5 _____

6 _____

7 _____

8 _____

9 _____

10 _____

Now, how much time and attention do your members with a '–' or a '– –' rating take from you?

 Here are some things to consider about trust:

People

- When leaders are good, employees trust them. When leaders are excellent, employees trust themselves.
- Trust is a normal thing when dealing with people: as trust is a risk, it is part of performance.
- When people talk about trust, it's always when it's missing. Its appearance is its non-existence.
- Trust does not work without trusting yourself – and this requires courage. Reducing control requires trust.

Leadership

- Eighty per cent of your attention and time will be taken up by the members of your team whom you don't trust.
- To achieve speed, leaders need to let go, trust and reduce control.
- Mistrust starts a demotivation spiral. It always starts with the leader and with low expectations, ignorance of competence, mistrust of accountability, the feeling that we know better than others and the tendency to over-control.
- Mistrust does not require justification. Trust requires justification.

Relationships

- Giving trust creates the duty to return it (reciprocal). It tends towards equilibrium. This means that trust has a price. More trust means less traditional control.
- People come to institutions but leave leaders. This says a lot about trust and relationships.

Systems

- The boundaries of trust are where the system collapses – this is where the organization is at risk.
- Trust increases speed, reduces transaction costs and builds commitment.
- With trust, there is no need to tweak systems to get things done. This reduces the time required to act.
- Trust as a control has low transaction costs. It works without the need for formal contractual agreements.
- Every commercial transaction requires trust.
- Trust is the only resource needed for survival in an economy of speed.
- It is not control that undermines trust. Trust needs control. Control is a prerequisite for trust. It is important to get that balance right.

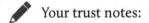 Your trust notes:

#11:
REVIEW
COMMITMENT

Commitment and trust are strongly related, and they are linked to the concept of 'give and take':

- **Take** is what stakeholders want from your organization (the needs the organization fulfils)
- **Give** is what stakeholders bring to your organization (the things they contribute that you want as an organization)

In an agile organization, trust requires both: the balance between give and take and the commitment to return the favour of giving and the benefit of taking. Ideally, give and take are in balance when the combination is in the trust and commitment space.

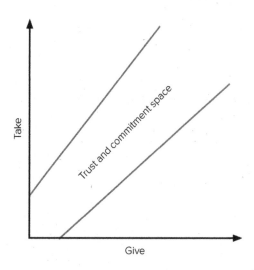

Here is your commitment test: use the following list of needs, what stakeholders want from you, and contributions, what you want from the stakeholders, to map out how trust creates commitment and value in your organization for every stakeholder group with the following stakeholder map.

Stakeholder	What they want	What you want from them
Employees	Purpose, care, skills and pay	Hands, hearts, minds and voices
Customers	Fast, right, cheap and easy	Profit, growth, opinion and trust
Investors	Returns, rewards, numbers and faith	Capital, credit, risk and support
Suppliers	Profit, growth, opinion and trust	Fast, right, cheap and easy
Supervision	Legality, fairness, safety and truth	Rules, reasons, clarity and advice
Communities	Jobs, fidelity, integrity and wealth	Image, skills, suppliers and support

The stakeholder map: Use the items in the stakeholder list to make a judgment of the balance between give and take.

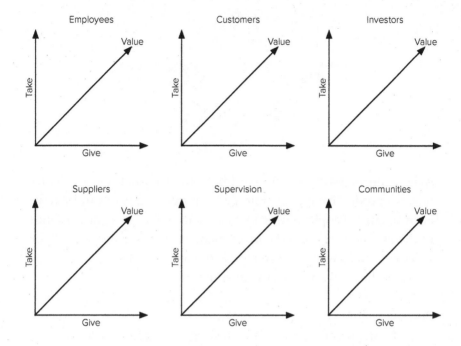

When your stakeholders' give and take are in balance, then you have passed the stakeholder test. You are in the zone of people-centric management. Are your stakeholders in balance? What have you learned?

#12:
CHECK YOUR ENERGY

Agile is an investment: an investment in attention and time that releases productive energy. Energy is limited and needs to be refuelled at times. People-centric management builds on a good balance of the use of energy and the investment in energy. Here is a test for you to use to gauge where you are with your energy.

Mark the answers that fit your situation:

Body:
- I don't regularly have enough sleep, and I often wake up tired
- I often skip meals or don't eat sufficiently
- I don't do perform sufficient physical activities
- I don't take frequent breaks to renew my energy

Mind:
- I have difficulty focusing on one thing and am often interrupted
- I spend a large portion of the day reacting on crises or short-term requests
- I don't take sufficient time for learning, thinking and fun things
- I often work long hours and don't take vacation

Emotions:
- I often feel irritated, impatient or limited by stress
- I don't have sufficient time for important relationships
- I have little time for my favourite activities
- I use little time to relax and enjoy my performance

Spirit:
- I don't spend time on work that uses all my talents
- What I consider important is not where I spend my time, attention and energy
- My work is determined by others rather than following my purpose
- I don't invest sufficient time and energy for social engagement

The number of marked answers is: _____
    0–3 Superb energy balance
    4–6 Reasonable energy balance
    7–10 Significant energy imbalance
    11–16 Energy is out of balance

What do you need to work on? Think about what you can do to refuel your energy. Use Tool #13, Refuel Your Energy.

#13:
REFUEL YOUR ENERGY

Agility requires energy, and energy requires renewal and refuelling. Make a plan to more frequently stop to refuel your energy with the following people-centric actions:

 Body: Which practices help you to mobilize your energy? Examples: nutrition, sports, sleep, etc.

 Emotions: Which practices help you to find a better quality of energy?
You can control your emotions and find positive energy through breathing, stories, purpose, etc.

Mind: How do stretch your potential and limit interference? Be aware. Focus your attention. Eliminate interference where you can.

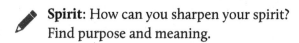 **Spirit**: How can you sharpen your spirit? Find purpose and meaning.

#14:
PAY ATTENTION

Agile depends on the capability to focus attention and focus of attention requires energy. Both are limited resources. That's why it makes sense to think about where you invest your attention.

Start by completing the first three columns in the table below.

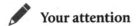 **Your attention**

What are the areas that require your attention?	Importance	Urgency	Priority
	1 2 3 4 5 6 7 8 9 10	1 2 3 4 5 6 7 8 9 10	
	1 2 3 4 5 6 7 8 9 10	1 2 3 4 5 6 7 8 9 10	
	1 2 3 4 5 6 7 8 9 10	1 2 3 4 5 6 7 8 9 10	
	1 2 3 4 5 6 7 8 9 10	1 2 3 4 5 6 7 8 9 10	
	1 2 3 4 5 6 7 8 9 10	1 2 3 4 5 6 7 8 9 10	
	1 2 3 4 5 6 7 8 9 10	1 2 3 4 5 6 7 8 9 10	
	1 2 3 4 5 6 7 8 9 10	1 2 3 4 5 6 7 8 9 10	

Then complete the fourth column to rank the areas in line with people-centric priorities. How much attention does each area require? What interference do you expect?

#15:
TIME ACCOUNTS

Agile combines effectiveness with efficiency. Time is a scarce resource. That's why you need to keep an account of it. Pick one month from your calendar and count up the number of hours you use on each of the areas below. Add your own areas as required.

🖊 **Your time**

Topics	Time (hours and minutes)	Details	Rank
Strategy			
Reporting			
Reviews			
Projects			
Crisis			
Admin			
People			
Finance			
Communications			
Team			
Social			
Total	------		

Then, in the fourth column, rank the areas according to how much time you spend on them. What are the five most important topics, tasks or decisions in your role? Do you invest your time the people-centric way?

#16:
101 ON EXECUTIVE TIME

Here are some essentials to consider on the use of your time. Use this as a checklist for your time investments.

 The 101 list

MANAGE YOUR MEETINGS

- Separate the operational from the strategic
- Focus on action not discussions
- Work through a meeting process and standard

FOLLOW YOUR RHYTHM

- Focus on relevant topics and activities
- Deal with changes as they come
- Align intent and resources

USE TIME EFFECTIVELY

- Maintain productive communications practices
- Effectively deal with interference, deviations and exceptions
- Create private, quiet and relaxing time

MANAGE INTERACTIONS

- Trust and delegate
- Respond to requests. Say no

BE AWARE AND
FOCUS ATTENTION

- Carefully invest your resources
- Balance performance, learning and enjoyment

ESTABLISH BOUNDARIES

- Be clear about what is out of scope
- Balance private and business

SET YOUR AGENDA

- Deal with commitments
- Enforce your agenda

#17:
PACE YOUR TIME

Time is a source of energy. Both time and energy are limited resources. That's why it makes sense to think about how you invest your time.

Start by completing the first three columns in the table below.

 **Your time**

What are the themes that require your time?	Importance	Urgency	Priority
	1 2 3 4 5 6 7 8 9 10	1 2 3 4 5 6 7 8 9 10	
	1 2 3 4 5 6 7 8 9 10	1 2 3 4 5 6 7 8 9 10	
	1 2 3 4 5 6 7 8 9 10	1 2 3 4 5 6 7 8 9 10	
	1 2 3 4 5 6 7 8 9 10	1 2 3 4 5 6 7 8 9 10	
	1 2 3 4 5 6 7 8 9 10	1 2 3 4 5 6 7 8 9 10	
	1 2 3 4 5 6 7 8 9 10	1 2 3 4 5 6 7 8 9 10	
	1 2 3 4 5 6 7 8 9 10	1 2 3 4 5 6 7 8 9 10	

Then complete the fourth column to rank the areas in line with your priorities. How much time does each area require? What interferences do you expect?

#18:
EXECUTIVE
PACE

People-centric managers take stock of how they use your time. Here are the things you need to think about:

 Your 'Here and Now.' Write five sentences about your organization.

Which time do you live in? Does your writing show the past, the present or the future?

 Your Agenda. How do you use your time? Do you follow your rhythm and flow, or do you create to do lists?

I found that those who create to-do lists use more time creating the list than getting things done. Time pressures and the need for schedules and deadlines limit creativity and continuity.

 Your Attention. What interrupts your time? How do you deal with it?

Be aware, time is a resource, not a limiting condition
 Your Flow. How do you think about your time?

Schedules and calendars limit our ability to plan and implement intelligent change.
 Your Rhythm. How do you schedule your time?

Organize your time in blocks. This leaves time for creativity and spontaneity.
 Your Effectiveness. How do you shape your time?

Use time as a continuity rather than a clock. Prevent routine from taking over.
 Your Patterns. What patterns do you follow? Are they helpful?

Patterns are events in time. Through time these events become meaning.

 Your Pace. What is your rhythm? Daily, weekly, monthly, annually? How can you influence it to your benefit?

Selecting the right rhythm is the key to any transformation in organizations. When you pick the right rhythm, energy will flow in your organization with less effort and improved relationships, emotions and performance. Watch out for your corporate rhythm.

 Your Momentum. How do you use special moments to your advantage?

The right momentum releases ample productive energy. Use the momentum when things change, new things happen rather than follow your timekeeper with predetermined habits, bureaucracy and control.

If you restarted your job today, what would you do? Take your time to think about your job and how you spend your time.

#19: ACCOUNTABILITY PROFILE

Agile builds on the accountability of individuals. The Accountability Profile establishes executive space. Here is the template for people-centric jobs. See Figure 39 for an example of a completed template.

JOB: CEO	
POSITION	**ACCOUNTABILITY**
Responsibility: Reports to: Control: Resources:	Metrics and results: Tasks: Rights:
COLLABORATION	**PROFILE**
Influence: Duties: Support for: Supported by:	**Span of control** Few resources ▬▬▬▬▬ Many resources **Span of accountability** Little choice ▬▬▬▬▬ Lots of choice **Span of influence** Within the organization ▬▬▬▬▬ Outside the organization **Span of support** Few support commitments ▬▬▬▬▬ Lots of support commitments

#20:
MAKE YOUR CHOICE

People with knowledge are executives; they make decisions. It is the duty and right of executives to make decisions.

With set rules, routines and tools, your organization guides much of the decision-making in your organization.

Complex and difficult decisions with consequences often come with the following: risk, confusion, doubts, mistakes, regrets, concerns and loss.

Feelings around decision-making may include the following: self-doubt, pressure, commitments, and worrying about the past and the future.

Agile requires that you follow people-centric principles with your choice.

Now, it is your time to make your choice of agile. Use these steps:

 What is your context?
- Fresh insights and information offer new perspectives
- Maintain your own perspective
- Understand what influences your decision
- Note all your concerns that you want to eliminate via the decision
- Separate out results and resources in the goal definition.
- Explain what you want to achieve with the decision

 Document your intent

What are the options?
- Options lead to better choices
- You can never choose an option that you have not considered
- Ask the 'why' this needs resolve
- Give your intuition time – and trust it
- Ask others for ideas – be open to conversations
- Find alternatives – be open to new, more, etc.

 Articulate your options

 What are the consequences?
- Imagine the future
- Understand the consequences
- Writing them down clears your mind
- Eliminate bad alternatives

 Articulate your consequences

How do you balance conflicting demands?
- Decisions with conflicting demands cannot be solved by just focusing on one demand
- There is never a perfect solution – it is always necessary to balance demands

 Articulate how you address your conflicting demands

 How do you mitigate the risks
- What are your most pressing risks?
- What are the most probable results of these risks?
- What is the probability that these risks will occur?
- What are consequences of every risk?
- Evaluate alternatives to mitigate these risks

 Articulate your risks and how you can mitigate them

#21:
START WITH
YOUR TEAM

Having made the choice of agile, it is time to share your idea with your team in three ways:

- Encourage others to participate in your awareness about agile
- Make your insights about agile visible to others
- Learn from others about your agile idea

 Engage your team

Create awareness: Take the perspective of others

What to do	What to say
Share your monitoring results, explain your observations, articulate the meaning you attach to the elements, state your assumptions about the levers.	Here is what I think about agile... Here is how I reached my assumptions...
Explain your assumptions.	I think the following about management and the organization...
Make your reasoning explicit: • Who is affected? • How will they be affected? • Why?	I came to this conclusion because of (interference, potential, outcomes) about our current results and potential agile capabilities...
Share examples of the idea.	Imagine that work, management, the organization, etc. is...

Share insights: Test your assumptions

What to do	What to say
Encourage others to explore your model, levers and elements.	What do you think about the idea?
Reveal the limits of your thinking.	Here are aspects where you might be able to help me better understand...
Listen, remain open and encourage other opinions and views.	Do you see it differently? How does this compare with your insights?

Learn from others: Engage your team

What to do	What to say
Gently walk others through the Argyris' Ladder of Inference (Argyris, 1990; Senge, 1990) – offer your reasoning.	What leads you to conclude that? Can you help me to understand?
Explain the reasons for your inquiry.	I am asking you about your assumptions and concerns here because...
Check your understanding of what you have heard.	Am I correct assuming you have said...?

NOTES

1. For an extensive review of VUCA, see Michel (2020).

2. For a detailed description of the tools, see Michel (2013, pp. 209, 249).

3. For more information on the Agile Diagnostics, see agilityinsights.net

4. For a detailed review of Visual Design Thinking, see Michel (2017).

5. This section heavily draws on the work of Timothy Gallwey, whom I was fortunate to get to know and with whom I have shared my organization's work. I especially draw on Gallwey (2000).

6. If you use the canvas in a workshop setting, then I suggest that you download it from www.agilityinsights.net and create a poster to work with. With the poster, everyone can follow and contribute to the latest thinking.

BIBLIOGRAPHY

Anzengruber, J. (2013). SKM, die Strategie des Erfolgs: das Kompetenzmanagement bei der Siemens AG. In Erpenbeck, J., von Rosenstiel, L. and Grote S. (eds.) *Kompetenzmodelle von Unternehmen: Mit praktischen Hinweisen für ein erfolgreiches Management von Kompetenzen*. Stuttgart: Schäffer-Poeschel, p. 315–327.

Argyris, C. (1991). Teaching smart people how to learn. *Harvard Business Review*, 69(3): 99–109.

Argyris, C. (1990). *Overcoming Organizational Defenses*. Boston: Allyn and Bacon.

Bruch, H. and Ghoshal, S. (2004). *A Bias for Action: How Effective Managers Harness Their Willpower, Achieve Results, and Stop Wasting Time*. Boston: Harvard Business School Press.

Clemens, J. K. and Dalrymple, S. (2005). *Time Mastery: How Temporal Intelligence Will Make You a Stronger Leader*. New York: Amacon.

Csikszentmihalyi, M. (1990). *The Psychology of the Optimal Experience*. New York: Harper & Row.

Deming, W. E. (1993). *The New Economics*. Cambridge: MIT Press.

Drucker, P. F. (1967). *The Effective Executive: The Definitive Guide to Getting the Right Things Done*. New York: Harper Business Essentials.

Gallwey, W. T. (2000). *The Inner Game of Work*. New York: Random House.

Habermas, J. (1988). *Moralbewusstsein und kommunikatives Handeln*. 3. Aufl. Frankfurt a M.

Hamel, G. (1998). Strategy innovation and the quest for value. *Sloan Management Review*, Winter: 7–14.

Hax, A. C. and Majluf, N. D. (1996). *The Strategy Concept and Process: A Pragmatic Approach*. New York: Palgrave.

Joiner, B. L. (1994). *Fourth Generation Management*. New York: McGraw Hill.

Klein, G. (2009). *Streetlight and Shadows*. Boston: MIT.

Mankins, M. (2004). Stop wasting valuable time. *Harvard Business Review*, September. Last accessed 23 April 2020. https://hbr.org/2004/09/stop-wasting-valuable-time.

March, J. G. (1991). Exploration and exploitation in organizational learning. *Organization Science*, 10(1): 299–316.

Michel, L. (2020). *People-Centric Management: How Leaders Use Four Levers to Bring Out the Greatness of Others*. London: LID Publishing.

Michel, L. (2017). *Management Design: Managing People and Organizations in Turbulent times* (2nd ed.). London: LID Publishing.

Michel, L. (2013). *The Performance Triangle: Diagnostic Mentoring to Manage Organizations and People for Superior Performance in Turbulent Times*. London: LID Publishing.

Michel, L., Anzengruber, J., Wölfe, M. and Hixson, N. (2018). Under what conditions do rules-based and capability-based management modes dominate? *Risks*, 6(2): 32.

Neely, A., Adams, C. and Kennerly, M. (2002). *The Performance Prism: The Scorecard for Measuring and Managing Business Success*. London: Financial Times/Prentice Hall.

Nold, H., Anzengruber, J., Michel, L. and Wölfle, M. (2018). Organizational agility: Testing validity and reliability of a diagnostic instrument. *Journal of Organizational Psychology*, 18(3): DOI 10.33423/jop.v18i3.1292.

Nooteboom, B. (1999). The combination of exploitation and exploration: How does it work? EGOS Colloquium, Knowledge and Organization Track, Warwick, 3–6 July.

Schwartz, T. and McCarthy, C. (2007). Manage your energy, not your time. *Harvard Business Review*, October. Last accessed 23 April 2020. https://hbr.org/2007/10/manage-your-energy-not-your-time.

Senge, P. M. (1999). *The Dance of Change*. New York: Doubleday.

Senge, P. M. (1990). *The Fifth Discipline*. New York: Doubleday.

Simons, R. (2005). *Levers of Organization Design: How Managers Use Accountability Systems for Greater Performance and Commitment*. Boston: Harvard Business School Press.

Simons, R. (1995). *Levers of Control: How Managers Use Innovative Control Systems to Drive Strategic Renewal*. Boston: Harvard Business School Press.

Simons, R. and Davila, A. (1998). How high is your return on management? *Harvard Business Review*, January–February. Last accessed 23 April 2020. https://hbr.org/1998/01/how-high-is-your-return-on-management.

Sprenger, R. (2007). *Das Prinzip Selbst-verantwortung: Wege zur Motivation*. Frankfurt a M: Campus.

Sprenger, R. (2007). *Vertrauen führt: Worauf es in Unternehmen ankommt*. Frankfurt a M: Campus.

Stacey, R. (2000). *Complexity in Management*. New York, NY: Routledge.

Tichy, M. N., and Bennis, W. E. (2007). Making judgement calls: The ultimate act of leadership. *Harvard Business Review*, October. Last accessed 23 April 2020. https://hbr.org/2007/10/making-judgment-calls.

Weick, K. (1995). *Sensemaking in Organizations*. London: Sage.

LIST OF ILLUSTRATIONS

Figure 1: Expectations   15

Figure 2: Business Strategy   18

Figure 3: Traditional Management   24

Figure 4: The New Context   24

Figure 5: The Individual and the Institution   25

Figure 6: Four Operating Modes   26

Figure 7: Determinants of Success   31

Figure 8: The People Dimension   37

Figure 9: Contrasting Knowledge Work   39

Figure 10: Assumptions About Work   40

Figure 11: Accountability vs. Responsibility   42

Figure 12: Sources of Motivation   43

Figure 13: The Organization Dimension   48

Figure 14: The Management Dimension   52

Figure 15: Four People-Centric Levers   53

Figure 16: Stakeholder Expectations   57

Figure 17: Purpose Modes   61

Figure 18: Relationships Modes   64

Figure 19: Collaboration Modes   67

Figure 20: The Operations Dimension   71

Figure 21: Mentoring Stages   77

Figure 22: Mentoring   78

Figure 23: The Canvas   80

Figure 24: Your Agile Choice   82

Figure 25: The Five Leadership Dimensions   84

Figure 26: Self 1 and Self 2   93

Figure 27: Three Personal Interactions   94

Figure 28: The Work Environment   98

Figure 29: Flow   101

Figure 30: Stress   103

Figure 31: Priorities   104

Figure 32: Flow – Where Are You?   106

Figure 33: Steps to Reach the Flow Zone   106

Figure 34: Sources of Interference   107

Figure 35: Resources   136

Figure 36: Focus and Energy   150

Figure 37: Time and Energy   156

Figure 38: Accountability Levers   162

Figure 39: Accountability Profile   164

Figure 40: Agile Decision-Making   178

Figure 41: The People-Centric Shift   187

Figure 42: The Agile Tipping Point   188

Figure 43: A Transformation   189

Figure 44: Diagnostic Mentoring   190

Figure 45: Interdependencies and Knowledge   191

Figure 46: Scaling and Individualizing   192

Figure 47: A Team Effort   194

Figure 48: Experiential Learning   204

Figure 49: Awareness, Insights and Learning   206

Figure 50: Make your Choice of Agile Work   209

ABOUT THE AUTHOR

Lukas Michel is the owner of Agility Insights AG, based in Switzerland, and CEO of AGILITYINSIGHTS.NET, a global network of experienced business mentors.

In addition to lecturing at universities, licensing his own agile mentoring methodology, writing on management issues and building his consulting network, Lukas is a business leader with a track record of balance sheet accountability in his work for global corporations in Europe and Asia.

Over the course of his 40-year career he has worked with executive teams around the world, focusing on management and agility for a diverse range of local, national and global organizations.

For the last 20 years, Lukas has been developing Diagnostic Mentoring, a methodology that offers diagnostics and a common framework and language for scaling capabilities across all organizational levels.

He holds an MS degree in management from North Carolina State University and bachelor's degrees in textile management and teaching.

Lukas is the author of *The Performance Triangle*, *Management Design*, *People-Centric Management* and *Agile by Choice*.

BOOK SUMMARY

Agility in business has become one of the most important management topics of recent times. The ability to create and respond to change in order to succeed in an uncertain and turbulent business environment is the essence of agile. Agile spans people and organizations. It's the dominant capability of effective leadership in a dynamic context. For agile to reach its full capacity, it needs to permeate organizations to establish leadership everywhere.

At its core, agile leadership is about people, with people-centricity being the mirror image of agile. The shift to agile starts with the leader who makes a deliberate choice to enable people rather than 'command and control.' The decision to shift to agile requires an experience which most executives don't have. Most leaders' experiences stem from control being the backdrop behaviour they have grown up with. Control always dominates agile and has infiltrated traditional organizations, limiting their ability to establish enabling leadership throughout.

This book is a practical workbook for leaders on their journey to achieving agility. Gentle nudges push leaders to make their decision and initiate their personal shift to agile. The book moves the conversation over agility into practice, exercising measures and techniques that will encourage leaders to adapt with changing times. To help leaders to make that personal shift, it offers ideas and tools to master agility in their organizations.

Designed to be sensible and self-reflecting, the book also includes an appendix of over 20 exercises that have been tried and tested with executives all over the world in their successful pursuit of agile. Leaders who have used the *Agile by Choice* exercises report to having crossed the Rubicon to people-centric and agile. With that experience, their organizations have established leadership everywhere.